ISBN: 978-0-692-18184-3 (paperback)
ISBN: 978-1-5323-8947-4 (ebook)
ISBN: 978-1-949709-32-2 (hardcover)

Visit the author's website at
WesBerryGroup.com
for more information

Published in the United States of America

by Green Dragon Services.

BOOKS BY WES BERRY

Motivational Leadership & Business Series

Big Things Have Small Beginnings: The Motivation
and Mindset that Build a $750-Million Business (Book 1)

Success Factors: Million-Dollar Concepts
that Work for Everyone (Book 2)

Master the Metaverse: Multi-Million Dollar Investment Opportunities (Book 3)

Business Quick Reads Series

The Positive Side of Golf: Motivation

Ice Cream Therapy: Mindset

Icons of Success: Leadership

The Ritz Experience: Growth and Scalability

Ty Cobb, Babe Ruth, and So On: Teamwork

The Right Stuff: Integrity

The Two Steves: Core Competencies

FUD Moneyball: Change

Get on Board: Inclusion

Stress Is My Superpower

Outcome Based Sales

Effective Communication

DEDICATION

This book is dedicated to my wife Mi and our four sons: Aaron, Brandon, Bradley, and Wes. Okay, so I am not the easiest person to live with, and they have endured an awful lot over the years. To my sons I'd like to publicly apologize for that incident with the elephant. And to my wife I apologize for the times we went sailing.

Also, to you the reader I dedicate this book in the hope that you will take some bits of knowledge from these pages, even if only in the validation of what you may already know. Get in the great game and you'll enjoy the ride of your life—honestly, it's an amazing game, that will make your life worthwhile.

And finally, to Commander Duncan, USNR, who excited my interest in strategic thinking.

Wes

Table of Contents

Introduction 1

PART I: Examining the Playing Field **5**

1. Ambition…For Better, or Worse?...................................7
2. The American Business Climate...................................25
3. Your "Why" Is a Must-Know!......................................33

PART II: The Challenge of Leadership **41**

4. Mapping the Journey 43
5. Time: Friend or Foe? 65
6. $60 Thousand Dollars to $750 Million Dollars 71
7. Know Your Working Tools! 115
8. Listen!…and Learn:
   Understanding Others.......................................131
9. Controlling the Battlefield!................................143

PART III: Seeking Out That Needle in the Haystack 161

10. Finding the Right People: Needle in the Haystack..............163

11. A Message to Garcia..169

12. The Playbook of Elbert Hubbard............................179

13. A Message to Garcia *IS* a Message to Leaders Today 191

14. Searching for Rowan: Creative Initiative 197

15. How to Know One When You See One................................213

16. How to Manage a "Rowan"....................................225

17. How to Keep a "Rowan"—Reward......................................241

Conclusion 247

About the Author 259

INTRODUCTION

I chose the title *Big Things Have Small Beginnings* for this book because I know that I'm living proof of that very truth.

But I've found that I was never alone in that. In fact, just about every successful person I've met—and I've been privileged to have met quite a few—and every successful leader I've studied, has in some way or another borne out the same truth. That is, successful people seem to spend a lot more time and energy on small things that unsuccessful people so often seem to neglect.

Did you ever hear the story about the blacksmith who brought down a kingdom? Seems he was being a little careless one day, and so he missed one of the nails in a single horseshoe. Just a little thing, right?

Well, as the story goes, it seems that horseshoe soon worked itself loose on a single hard ride, and the poor horse stumbled and fell. He threw his rider, who was injured badly enough that he wasn't able to complete his journey. Unfortunately, that meant that the message the rider was carrying never got through to the general for whom it was intended. Had the general received the message in time, he would have waited just that one more day to attack, that is, until the large band of reinforcements

1

could arrive. He didn't know. So he did attack, as well as he was able. He felt he had no choice, and, sad to say, he was resoundingly defeated. But worse, he was the last and best defense of the king. And so the king, and of course the kingdom, was lost.

Man, if only that blacksmith had paid a little more attention to that seemingly minor detail.

And that's pretty much what this book is about.

I'm here to tell you that, when you take care of the little stuff, the big stuff has a really nice way of taking care of itself. And what I hope to accomplish in these few pages is to help you take better care of all that little stuff.

I've enjoyed a wonderful measure of success, both in my business and in my life, and I sincerely want the same for you. But it certainly wasn't always an easy road to travel. My hope is that, if you too are starting out on that road, or maybe are already well along the way and perhaps have hit a couple of ruts, then what I'm about to tell you might be of assistance to you on your own journey—in your business—and in your life.

Life is so doggone short. And it's so doggone precious when we're able to live it at a high level, a life of success, a life that's full of the deep joy that comes with working toward and accomplishing very worthwhile goals that make our lives, and the lives of those all around us, just a little bit better for our being here. It doesn't get any better than that. As far as I can see, if you learn to play in the great game of business, you will also be learning how to play in the great game of life.

I can't thank you enough for picking up this book. You're the kind of person who makes this country, and this world, a much better place for the ambition you have already shown. I'm pullin' for you. I really am. How I wish we had many more like you.

Soooo, how about we get started?

PART I

Examining the Playing Field

The person who starts out simply with the idea of getting rich won't succeed; you must have a larger ambition. There is no mystery in business success. If you do each day's task successfully, and stay faithfully within these natural operations of commercial laws which I talk so much about, and keep your head clear, you will come out all right.

John D. Rockefeller

Chapter 1—Ambition...

For Better, or Worse?

Let's begin our discussion with "Ambition." Nothing in business will get accomplished without it. You simply can't play in the great game without ambition.

Ambition is an absolute essential. But make no mistake, for better or worse, genuine ambition involves struggle. We set out to achieve something that we believe is really worthwhile. And it is the achievement of that worthwhile goal that brings us a genuine sense of our own worth. We make a difference. We earn our dignity. But let me add that the very struggle itself, even in the absence of the success we set out to achieve, brings much of the same benefit to us. *It makes us people with a purpose.*

Ambition also puts considerable demands on us. It requires a whole lot more of us than just our lofty "ambitions," our dreams in life. It requires a toughness of mind and spirit that only really grows in us once we enter the ring, once we begin to play in the great game. And success is guaranteed to no one.

But if you're not willing to lose, you shouldn't be playing

the game.

What is ambition?

For most people the term is a little ambiguous, isn't it? You're sitting at your desk shootin' the breeze over morning coffee with a co-worker, and your department head walks by.

"She's ambitious," you say.

Is it a compliment? Or is it a castigation? The answer to that question depends largely on whether or not you consider yourself to be ambitious, and for what reason—that is, to what end. And be assured that this discussion is not a new one.

Seventeenth-century philosopher, statesman, and jurist Sir Francis Bacon pondered this same point in his essay *On Ambition* (1612). In his now-archaic English, he writes:

> *So ambitious men, if they find the way open for their rising, and still get forward, they are rather busy than dangerous; but if they be checked in their desires, they become secretly discontent, and look upon men and matters with an evil eye, and are best pleased, when things go backward; which is the worst property in a servant of a prince, or state.*

Well isn't that clear as a bell? But, in fact, it sure does ring true!

He's saying that when ambitious men are allowed to engage in their passion, they become marvelously busy and industrious. They get stuff done! Contrary to common suspicion, he says, they do not become dangerous. On the contrary, he adds, the danger of ambition usually arises when such men are denied the pursuit of their ambitions, and then become a veritable danger to society, primarily out of the frustration and the consequent bitterness that follows. Rather than steering their formidable energies toward the good of society, they instead channel them toward its damage and destruction. This, of course, is particularly onerous when such frustrated men are servants of a prince, or of a state. Cautiously, Bacon instructs princes to manage ambitious people and channel their activities such that their creativity and ambitions are given breath, if not even wings.

> *Therefore it is good for princes, if they use ambitious men, to handle it, so as they be still progressive and not retrograde; which, because it cannot be without inconvenience, it is good not to use such natures at all.*

In the plain English of today, he's suggesting that, if ambitious—and therefore productive—people cannot have their ambitions nurtured by the activities for which they have been enlisted, then it would be much better never to have enlisted such people at all, so that their frustrated ambition doesn't end up frustrating the success of a venture.

More than a few business writers have drawn parallels between the characteristics required for success in business with those required for success in war. With certain obvious limitations, it makes sense. The challenge, in both war and in business, of pitting oneself against fierce competitors, merely scratches the surface.

Bacon addresses this as well, but points out that an overly ambitious man may crave the *accolades* of greatness more than the doing of the great thing for the right reasons. He might report success where none existed solely for his own advancement.

An overly ambitious military officer might look forward to chaos. Chaos might well be his opportunity for advancement! He would crave the opportunities that battle presents. He might even wager selfishly with the lives under his command.

And then, if his misguided ambition really grabs a hold of him to where he starts to lose control, being acutely aware of the opportunity that chaos could bring, such a man might go so far as to create the chaos himself, regardless of the wisdom of his battlefield decisions, and particularly regardless of the sacrifice of the lives of his soldiers. As his opportunity lies in chaos, he could look to create such an environment for his own advantage.

And ambitious people know well the maxim, "The greater the risk, the greater the rewards." If successful, therefore, making risky wagers might seem the thing to do. Taken to the extreme, advancement by assassination might even be within the character of this type of individual. Hmmm, talk about ambition gone awry, right?

There's little doubt but that an openly ambitious man in the military is a recipe for disaster. As such, these very ambitions will block the achievements that an ambitious man strives for. Is it any wonder that highly ambitious individuals are almost chronically beset with dissatisfaction? In a military structure, this trait could lead to real complications.

Balance

The trick is to have just the right amount of ambition. The "Goldilocks" zone of ambition is ideal for a military career. Too little ambition and nothing gets done; too much and you are constantly discontent, leading to unwise or dangerous actions that could prove disastrous. Just the right measure of modest ambition, and you've got the perfect recipe for a truly effective and trusted officer.

The great Chinese General and war strategist, Sun Tzu, victorious in battle after battle back in the 6th century BC, elaborated on this quandary with his *The Art of War*, certainly one of the greatest books ever written. Even today, it is studied in virtually all military academies. And now the business world has grown well aware of the application of Sun Tzu's war principles and practices to the current art of business.

As the great general says, "In the midst of chaos, there is also opportunity." And yet, while Sun Tzu recognized the impact of this principle, he also clearly cautioned military leaders to maintain a discerning eye over an overtly ambitious man, one who could abuse a chaotic condition to advance his personal glory rather than for true battlefield success.

I've got to agree with Sun Tzu. It is entirely true that some are simply too ambitious to serve in the military. I'd rather say that some are not meant for a peacetime military; although I would prefer to say that some have an affinity for audacity, a willingness to take surprisingly bold risks. In the words of Fredrick the Great "L'audace, l'audace, toujours l'audace," or, as translated and re-quoted by WWII's outstandingly-successful war leader General George Patton, "Audacity, audacity, always audacity!"

Let's face it. Ambition is a powerful sword, and appreciably so when it's wielded by a person of integrity. When it is associated with a few individuals who are unafraid to openly strive for success, the results can be substantial.

Timing

There is one key factor which may be largely out of your hands: timing. Perhaps it is all about timing—when you are born and when you come of age. If the skills and traits you possess are in need, and your course is set to take the greatest advantage, then you can achieve what you were born to be.

Don't get me wrong. I'm not talking about little things here. If you believe you are meant for greatness, and refuse to let failures distract you, then you can achieve great things. And these great things will advance not only yourself, but those around you. In fact, with an additional touch of good fortune, you may well end up advancing Society or Mankind itself primarily as a result of your intrepid audacity!

When an outlier happens to possess the physical and mental strengths required, and has the audacity to act boldly with his or her ambitions, in the right place at the right time…well…this is the making of a Caesar. And it was owing to the ambition of a Caesar that the greatness of Rome was born.

Julius Caesar

Greatness? You bet. It was none other than Julius Caesar (100-44BC), and his immediate successors Augustus (63BC-14AD) and Tiberius (42BC-37AD), who converted the early Republic of Rome into the mighty Roman Empire, ushering in the *Pax Romana* (Latin for "Roman Peace"), a period of relative peace and prosperity that lasted throughout the known world of that time for over 200 years. To date, this is the longest period of widespread general peace the world has ever known.

Look at the words spoken by Shakespeare's Marc Antony (83-30BC), a Roman general and statesman who also played a significant role in the birth of the Empire, words chosen partly to eulogize his admired friend Julius Caesar following Caesar's assassination by another once-close associate, Brutus:

> *The noble Brutus hath told you Caesar was ambitious: If it were so, it was a grievous fault; And grievously hath Caesar answer'd it... Come I to speak at Caesar's funeral. He was my friend, faithful and just to me: But Brutus says he was ambitious; And Brutus is an honorable man.*

Yes, Caesar was ambitious for himself, but also for his friends and for Rome. You might ask how this can be, for ambition is thought of as greed. I tell you ambition, greed, and all the baser forms—thought of as the darker side of human nature—are simply tools. Like a gun. In the hands of a criminal, a gun affects society with pain. But, that same gun in the hand of the hero protects the innocent, and enforces the security that society requires to conduct the gentrification of its citizens.

Caesar's identity was Rome, and so his ambition was for Rome. What greater gift than audacious ambition for the citizens of Rome? And even in death did his efforts continue to work to unify Rome. To be sure, his legacy took about 80 years to usher in the *Pax Romana;* but many have argued persuasively that it was, in fact, Julius Caesar's death that began the long-term unification of Rome.

Granted, much blood was spilled for Rome to be Rome, and, true, justice and security were reserved mostly to those who were Roman citizens. Still, in the provinces it was better than it had been. The fall of Rome just before 400AD began the onset of the Dark Ages, and the consequent loss of the amazing peace, stability, and protection of its citizenry that were such hallmarks of the Empire. The eventual downfall of the Roman Empire was clearly a great loss to all mankind. And it would be another 500-1,000 years before the Dark Ages would finally come to a close, and the world could again pick itself up and begin to shine a little brighter light on itself.

So was Caesar an ambitious man? I'm sure he was. It's certainly fair to say that Caesar played at the very top of the great game. And all mankind should thank him for his ambition. He had the audacity to be ambitious, and the mindfulness to use these traits to impose his willfulness to unite his countrymen.

Was he perfect? Hardly. But, even with all his faults, and all of Rome's faults and limitations, the ambition and greed of Rome evolved into the audacity to force the peace. Yes, the desire of greed enforced the peace.

How, you might ask, can this be? Simple. Peace was the ambition of Caesar, and it was the ultimate ambition of Rome. Because with security comes prosperity, and the greed of Rome created prosperity. Sure, it was imperfect, as all institutions made by man inevitably are plagued with imperfections. However, with Rome, life was grander and better than what the world was without it. Rome changed the world from one of relentless tribal barbarism to one of organized, cooperative civilization. The societal revolution it ushered in, made possible by the force of the *Pax Romana*, brought advancements to the civilization of humankind that are practicably impossible to sketch out in full.

Keep in mind, the goal of every military commander is victory, and with victory there is peace.

So in *"Understanding Ambitious People,"* it's important to consider the necessary circumstances of the times in which you deal. But, as we've said, ambition is a powerful force. Therefore, in the absence of the engagement of war, it is clear that soldiers—those ambitious souls biting at the bit for action—must be kept busy, even when little of crucial importance is to be done. In days of old, the Army, in times of peace, would often be put to building roads, bridges, and other such useful tasks. Okay. Not bad. Not war, to be sure. But a pretty useful and practical means to occupy those ambitious soldiers in a constructive pursuit.

Need we look very far to see the effects of our not heeding these principles today?

How about all those dedicated, self-sacrificing—read "ambitious for peace and freedom"—soldiers in Iraq and Afghanistan who fought beside our own American troops to secure some measure of peace, tranquility, and future prosperity for their own families and countrymen following the close of the Iraq war? We were able to work with a lot of these former soldiers to help them work with us to improve their country, from infrastructure repairs and improvements to governing. But we simply couldn't work with all of them. Those who had to be overlooked became just what we're talking about here; ambitious men who, in defeat, were left without a means to fulfill their ambitions. These soldiers, trained in the arts of war, were left without a feeling of usefulness. Is it any wonder so many ended up becoming part of an insurgent force? Is it any wonder that they took out their frustrations using the skills they had acquired? Is it really any wonder they set about inflicting so much disruption to what should have been a lasting peace?

Perhaps the peace could have been maintained, however, if these men could have had their ambition channeled into tasks, albeit challenging, that they themselves could see as moving them in the direction of that lasting peace. Even a fool's errand would have avoided the damage that they inflicted on that troubled land.

If you're worried about your own ambition, pause a minute. Especially if you're worried about risk and about failure…well, then join the group. We all face it. If you're concerned that maybe you just don't have the critical leadership traits to be successful in the great game, maybe you're right—for now. But I'm here to tell you that all of what you need can be learned. It's the learning, the relentless attention to the small beginnings that will make all the difference. And those small things are often incredibly challenging.

Take some encouragement from the words of President Teddy Roosevelt. In his speech at the Sorbonne in Paris (April 23, 1910), he famously proclaimed:

> *It is not the critic who counts; not the man who points out how the strong man stumbles, or where the doer of deeds could have done them better. The credit belongs to the man who is actually in the arena, whose face is marred by dust and sweat and blood; who strives valiantly; . . . who at best knows in the end the triumph of high achievement, and who at worst, if he fails, at least fails while daring greatly.*

For Julius Caesar, the moment of decision probably came on January 10, 49BC at the river Rubicon, the boundary line between Gaul and the Roman Republic. By crossing this minor river, everyone knew, Caesar was leading his legions into a civil war in his beloved Rome. He uttered the famous phrase "alea iacta est ("the die has been cast"). And today, the phrase "crossing the Rubicon" has since come to mean passing "the point of no return." At that moment he knew that he was risking it all on a roll of the dice.

A Word About Risk

So, what drives a person to take such a monumental risk? What type of ambition must a man have to put his very life, and all

19

that he has achieved in that life to date, on the line? For Caesar, it's pretty clear that his ambition on that fateful day was fueled, at the very least, by his ambition to reform the city he loved. He clearly believed he could govern more wisely than the current government, and history has borne out that wisdom. Did he have personal ambitions for his own greatness? For his own place in the history of the world? I suppose he did. In fact, I can't imagine that he did not, at least in some way. But where does that come from? I'd say it comes from a mountain of self-knowledge, a ton of self-confidence, and years of challenging oneself to develop the skills necessary to carry out that ambition.

At that point, it might be better said that, given what he saw before him in Rome, and given who he had become himself, it might have been more unthinkable for him to have suppressed that ambition to reform his Rome. As you can see, ambition can require a willingness to roll the dice, especially if you have a notion that those dice just might be loaded in your favor.

There's always a chance you'll fall flat on your face. There's always that chance that you'll embarrass yourself, that you'll end up spending countless hours and every dime you can beg, borrow, or steal to fulfill that relentless ambition of yours. And there's always that chance that it'll bring you to abject failure, to the loss of your former financial stability, maybe even to the tragic loss of your friends, and heaven forbid, even your family. Yes, you could fail.

But here's the rub: If you're not willing to lose, you're not allowed to play in the game.

There is no one alive who has been successful who did not have failures! So, at least to start, you're in pretty good company. BUT, the critical lesson here is that people who were successful _learned from_ those same failures. So very often it was those classrooms of failure that, once their powerful lessons were learned, led to their success. They had learned to play in the great game.

With every opportunity, there is also risk. And with risk, by definition, there is always the possibility of loss. It takes guts to wrap ourselves around that.

But here's the good news. For all practical purposes, there is no risk that is insurmountable. And the immense depth of satisfaction you receive is often equal to the amount of risk you take.

Lets face it. If success was devoid of risk, if success took us down a path of ease and comfort, well then everybody else would be there too!

There's no question that I'm thankful to God for the wonderful blessings I've enjoyed. But when I say that, I'm saying that I'm thankful for stuff that He's given me that I know He's also given to just about everyone else on the planet too. And, as we'll see in our next chapter, He's especially given a whole bunch of great stuff to anyone who's living in this rather amazing capitalist democracy we call the United States of America.

America – the Land of Ambitious People

If you're looking to start and run a business—large or small —there is simply nowhere else on earth that you will have the same advantages and opportunities as you will in this country of ours.

Let me flesh that out a little bit.

It might be reasonably argued that throughout our history America has been the most "ambitious" country in the world.

I know what you're thinking. Hmmm, that word "ambition." As I mentioned earlier, for some people it puts a lousy taste in their mouth. We've all known people who are so ambitious that they think nothing of stepping on whomever and whatever they need to just so they can get what *they* want. Some politicians come to mind, right? How about a couple of your favorite dictators? Hitler was a pretty ambitious guy, don't you think? Yeah, and that makes him pretty loathsome, right?

But wait a minute. If ambition in its purest form is "an eager or strong desire to achieve something," (thank you, Mr. Webster!), then maybe we ought to be looking at a few other models of ambition too…you know, just to be fair to the word and maybe round this thing out.

George Washington had a pretty strong ambition to establish the world's very first government by and for its people. And he and his Founding Father compatriots exercised that ambition at the very risk of their respectable fortunes, their personal comfort, and ultimately at the risk of their lives. Abraham Lincoln had an unbelievably strong ambition to unite a divided country even while eradicating its widespread practice of slavery, upon which half the country's economy heavily rested.

And how about Henry Ford? When you get a chance, take a closer look at the risks that guy took! The obstacles that fell across his path! That was some remarkable ambition, to say the very least.

It's certainly fair to say that astronauts are ambitious too. Like Kirk, they want to "boldly go where no one has gone before." How about doctors? How else could anybody endure that much concentrated education—let alone ridiculously high insurance premiums—without a couple bucketsful of ambition ?

Ambition is like money. It in itself is pretty neutral. It's up to us to use it to do good…or not. But you know what? If you really have a desire to succeed in your business, it is absolutely going to take ambition—that is, the really good kind.

Let's be clear here: your very desire to succeed _IS_ your ambition. Embrace it! Without ambition, your chances of success in business are pretty slim.

As we've seen in this chapter, ambition is what gives us the people who move our world forward. It's behind our Julius Caesars, our Franklin D. Roosevelts, and it's even behind every runner who ever set out one day to finally train for and complete that elusive 26-mile, 385-yard marathon.

And the absence of ambition? Well, we've all known our share of couch potatoes, haven't we?

In conclusion, know this: truly ambitious people would rather taste defeat than never have the chance to wear the laurel wreaths of victory. And the best ambitions are not just for oneself, but for an ideal, something greater than the individual.

Chapter 2—The American
Business Climate

If you're an American reading this in the 21st century, consider yourself very lucky. You might say privileged, in fact. Y'know, the world's a lot smaller today than it ever was before. And it seems to shrink a little more every year. The elevator's getting crowded going up to the penthouse suite, and there are a whole lot of different languages, and the political and business philosophies that go with them, riding up there alongside us.

Because of the internet, and of the ease and fluidity of worldwide multinational commerce, our competition is not simply just within our own country anymore. We compete today with nations that may be very different from our own. Some are Democratic and capitalist, some are Communist, a couple others are Socialist, and it seems that more and more of them every year are essentially military dictatorships. If you're setting out to start, or to prosper in a business in the United States of America, well, I'd say you've dodged a bullet. You've got a lot better shot of success here than just about any other place on the planet.

Did you ever wonder why the U.S. seems to be so head and shoulders above so much of the rest of the economic pack? Certainly our democracy is not yet quite perfect. Ahem. And our capitalism has its bumps and grinds as well, don't we all know. In fact, many today would argue that our government is all screwed up! They can't agree on anything! Nothing gets done because there's way too much arguing going on, and way too little decision-making!

So, are we really all that lucky to be doing business as Americans?

Without a doubt, I'd say yeah. You bet. In fact, I'd say it's the underpinning foundation of our governmental system that keeps my optimism up, that assures me that there is no place else in the world where a business mind can have a greater potential for success than right here.

I'm not here to offer some half-baked lesson in politics or economics, but please allow me to illustrate one small, but very key part of this hope that burns so brightly in me. It's certainly one of the cornerstones of my—and your—ability to be successful. Don't take it from me, though! Take it instead from a bona fide expert in the workings of our rather unique government.

American Exceptionalism

The late Supreme Court Justice Antonin Scalia served our country in that capacity from 1986 until his surprising and lamentable death in 2016. Of the roughly three hundred million citizens in this country, only nine of us are selected to ensure that the ship is being steered with an even keel through some mighty turbulent waters. I think it's fair to say they are our bona fide experts in the Constitution, the structure of our government, and in our legacy of democracy and capitalism. So don't listen to *me* on this; listen instead to what a greatly-respected stalwart member of this very select company has to say. Yes, it will take a second of your reading time, but I hope you'll find that second to be well-spent.

This is an excerpt from Justice Scalia's *Opening Statement to Congress on American Exceptionalism* (October 5, 2011). He tells the members of Congress that he has the frequent occasion to speak to high school, college, and some of the finest post-graduate law students in the country.

> ...So, when I speak to these groups the first point I make— I ask them, "What do you think is the reason that America is such a free country?" "What is it in our Constitution that makes us what we are?"
> The answer would be: freedom of speech, freedom of the press, no unreasonable searches and seizures, no

quartering of troops in homes -- those marvelous provisions of the Bill of Rights.

But then I tell them, if you think that a bill of rights is what sets us apart, you're crazy. Every banana republic in the world has a bill of rights. Every President for life has a bill of rights. The bill of rights of the former "Evil Empire," the Union of Soviet Socialist Republics, was much better than ours. I mean it, literally. It was much better. We guarantee freedom of speech and of the press -- big deal. They guaranteed freedom of speech, of the press, of street demonstrations and protests; and anyone who is caught trying to suppress criticism of the government will be called to account. Whoa, that is wonderful stuff!

Of course -- just words on paper, what our Framers would have called a parchment guarantee. And the reason is, that the real Constitution of the Soviet Union -- you think of the word "constitution," it doesn't mean a "bill"; it means "structure"; [when] you say a person has a sound "constitution," [he] has a sound "structure." The real Constitution of the Soviet Union, which is what our Framers debated that whole summer in Philadelphia in 1787—they didn't talk about the Bill of Rights; that was an afterthought, wasn't it?—that Constitution of the Soviet Union did not prevent the centralization of power, in one person or in one party. And when that happens the game is over; the Bill of Rights is just what our Framers would call a parchment guarantee…

…So, the real key to the distinctiveness of America is the structure of our government…

…One part of it, of course, is the independence of the judiciary; but there's a lot more…

...And I hear Americans saying this nowadays, and there's a lot of it going around. They talk about a "dysfunctional government" because there's disagreement. And the Framers would have said, yes, that's exactly the way we set it up. We wanted this to be power contradicting power...

...So, unless Americans can appreciate that and learn to love the separation of powers, which means learning to love the gridlock, which the Framers believed would be the main protection of minorities—the main protection. If a bill is about to pass that really comes down hard on some minority [and] they think it's terribly unfair, it doesn't take much to throw a monkey wrench into this complex system.

So, Americans should appreciate that and they should learn to love the gridlock. It's there for a reason -- so that the legislation that gets out will be good legislation.

And thus conclude my opening remarks.

To my mind, what Justice Scalia is telling us is that we have a choice: to live with the continual congressional verbal wrestling match we call gridlock, or to live in an essentially totalitarian state. Perhaps like you, I used to bellyache about the gridlock in Washington, and in a lot of state and local governments too! But I don't much anymore. I recognize that it's a pretty healthy sign that I've found the right place to conduct my business. So have you.

Justice Scalia titled his brief remarks *American Exceptionalism*. That's a term that was thrown around an awful lot back in the political campaigns of the early 2000s. It's often attributed to Alexis de Tocqueville, the French elite philosopher writer who famously toured our fledgling country and wrote about his impressions, highly positive, in his popular work, *Democracy in America* (1835). The problem is de Tocqueville never actually used that term. Yeah, he did say America was an "exceptional nation" with a role to play in history.

But the term "exceptionalism" was actually a derisive label given to us by none other than one of the Communist world's most murderous, despotic pioneers, Josef Stalin! He was enraged, apparently, that one of his marketing disciples was so unsuccessful in spreading Communism through America even in the midst of the Great Depression of the 1930s.

Too bad, huh? Well, for Communism, anyway. But hats off to Americans.

American Exceptionalism—not Stalin's, but the good kind —means that everyone who is willing to do what needs to be done can be a remarkable success. But people have to actively make the decision that they want to rise to that position. It has been my experience that those who disagree with this are simply looking for an excuse for not doing what is necessary. The real freedom that American Exceptionalism champions is the freedom of upward mobility. Yes, it does take work. But if one is willing to do that work, then that mobility, that position, is waiting for you; it's pulling for you to reach it.

Chapter 3—Your "Why" Is a Must-Know!

Why are you doing this?

You're reading this because you want to run a business more efficiently. Maybe it's YOUR business! Or, maybe you're responsible for a significant (or small) part of the success of someone else's business.

Maybe you play a relatively small part in a world-class automaker conglomerate, and your responsibility is to ensure that the assembly line in your small town is continually supplied with grease, and you have to organize and schedule the four of your maintenance guys who do that for the rest of the plant.

Ultimately, it doesn't really matter what it is you do. Regardless of your role in your enterprise, it's critical that you decide *why* you're doing what you do. The great game *IS* a great game, but only if you know in your heart of hearts why you're playing in it.

Does it seem too basic to you? Okay, I guess on the surface it might. But it's important to know.

When things get tough—as they do nearly every day—its your "why" that'll get your out of bed in the morning.

Discovering Your Why

You're working, I'd imagine, because you want to make money. Okay…*why*? Do you want to be the richest guy on the block? Are you looking to retire at age 40 with an appreciable nest egg, on a beach in Costa Rica for the second half of your life? Do you want to provide for your family so that those brief twenty years spent together with your children will yield a bunch of keepsake memories?

Maybe you've decided to work your buns off until you create genuine financial "abundance." You are setting out to eliminate any financial stresses for your loved ones.

Or maybe, like a lot of folks, you're working to make ends meet month to month, and hopefully to help your kids get through college at the end of it all.

Something to think about, right?

But there's another dimension to that "why."

Why are you in that *particular* business? What keeps you in it today? If you're an entrepreneur, a business owner, what made you decide to make your living with that particular product or service? What do you hope to accomplish? In other words, how are you going to play this great game? Which talents and abilities of yours are you going to focus on? Where do you hope to make your mark in the game? And then…*why*?

Are you setting out to change the world with a creation that you yourself invented? Are you hoping to streamline the public's use of some product or service in whole new ways, formerly unthought-of, and haul in boatloads of cash by doing so? Is it important to you that what you offer your community, or maybe this world, improves some facet of our existence?

Hmmm, sorta lofty, eh? I don't mean to get all flowery and romantic on you here, but I do think these questions make a difference—a *big* difference. Because business is tough. The great game would simply not be all that great if it were easy. Competition is always fierce. And there is never any success without a mountain of obstacles, mishaps, setbacks, and abject failures. And in times like that, if you're relying solely on your grits and guts and bare-knuckles perseverance, I think you run the risk of burning out.

When things get tough, it's your "why" that'll keep you going. It's your "why" that will sit you down with your best people to relentlessly brainstorm what it's going to take to move the business just one more step forward. It's your "why" that will justify risk. And it's your "why" that will get you to grit your teeth every single month and pay those horrendous bills even as you continue to drive on ahead.

My own "Why?" I keep a picture of my wife and my four sons on my desk. They're the very biggest part of my "why," as I'm fairly sure your family is for you.

I'll mention again that I can tell you it is the many small things you do that will make the big things happen. But, if you cannot muster the enthusiasm, the passion, for taking on each of those small things, it's very likely that the big things will never get done. And it's the "WHY" that will supply you with that critical passion to get those small things done.

But I've been fortunate to have enough success that I've been able to offer some significant financial help to a number of local charities that I care about as well. If you've been in that position too, then you know how genuinely heartwarming it is to see so many good people in need benefiting directly by something you've been able to contribute to their lives. Maybe you've been the one to offer someone that critical leg-up in their life situation, maybe in their educational pursuits, or maybe in their pursuit of a challenging career. If you have, then you too know the depth of the feelings that course through your blood when you get to witness the positive impact of your life on someone else's. There's really no need for a formal "thank you," is there?

I can only imagine, for example, what someone like Bill Gates or Warren Buffet must feel when the success they have achieved actually changes the course of health and education throughout the greater part of the continent of Africa. Their financial contributions and organizational focus have wrestled to the ground what was arguably the most devastating health crisis on that continent, AIDS. That's one helluva "why!"

My business was flowers. I may not have had the seemingly bottomless bank accounts of Bill and Warren, but I did have access to a lot of flowers.

And every year I got to make a fairly powerful statement with those flowers. I passed out roses, for free, to anyone who would like one, every January to celebrate the legacy of Dr. Martin Luther King. That's right. They were free. Anyone could come into any of our stores and ask for a free rose, or maybe even a dozen of them, and we'd give them to them. In fact, we gave tens of thousands of them out every single year, and more than 200,000 overall, a dozen at a time. And we gave them out with the request that each recipient might keep one, but then pass out the rest of them to friends, or maybe even to strangers, as a celebration of diversity and community in honor of Dr. Martin Luther King, a legacy that I strongly feel we needed to keep alive, and it made me feel alive just to be able to make some concrete contribution to that effort.

I suppose if my "why" was to make a lot of money, you might think this may not be the best way to go about it. We'll come back to this in a later chapter. But let me at least say here that I find it easy to justify this kind of significant expenditure when I know that it conforms to a broad "why" that I've created for myself.

I recall driving up to one of my franchise stores and watching customer after smiling customer, men and women both, walking out with a beautiful rose in their hand. Many of them had apparently come in for nothing else! And you know what? I was delighted! I found myself smiling too, about the impact this would have on good people. And I did NOT at all worry about the expense it was going to cost my company. It conformed to a big "why" that I had fought long and hard to achieve.

I guess I'd have to acknowledge that I've been blessed with pretty good success for my business efforts. And that success has allowed me, over the years, to offer significant financial and volunteer assistance to philanthropic causes like autism, racial and ethnic integration, and to a wide variety of others' business struggles, to name just a few.

It's like looking at that family photo on my desk. It's another one of those things that gives me energy when I crawl out of the sack every morning.

You have to find your "why," because you're going to need it if you really want to get serious about learning to play the great game.

PART II

The Challenge of Leadership

You are a bus driver. The bus, your company, is at a standstill, and it's your job to get it going.
... In fact, leaders of companies that go from good to great start not with "where" but with "who." They start by getting the right people on the bus, the wrong people off the bus, and the right people in the right seats.

Jim Collins

Chapter 4—Mapping the Journey

I absolutely loved taking my family on vacation. When your children are growing up, you only have a small window of time, but it's a precious window that offers some wonderful opportunities. You can offer your children the kinds of experiences that they'll enjoy and remember for the rest of their lives. And these times will truly contribute to the makeup of their childhood.

You never know what you're going to see or encounter along the way. And sometimes, if time permits, it's pretty cool to stop off and check out something your kids stumbled upon on some highway billboard—a museum, a reptile zoo, maybe what's touted as the largest ball of yarn in the world! Who would ever want to miss that, right? However, with a little research, you can also make sure to be in Hawaii at the height of the whale migration, or maybe be in Chichen Itza for the equinox!

But I've got to tell you, we love just looking around too, at the countryside, at a city we happen to be passing through, or maybe even a quaint little town with those cute overloaded flower baskets hanging from every light post on main street. We really enjoy the journey.

We may head out from Michigan for a road trip to Washington, D.C. But along the way maybe we'll come across a Civil War battlefield—Gettysburg comes to mind—and we just might decide to sidetrack some to add a little gusto to our journey. In fact, it might well be part of our goal to keep our eyes open for just such a diversion, because one of our sub-goals was to make this an educational trip, anyway.

At the same time, we keep heading in the direction of our designated destination. That's our goal, and everything else we do on that trip really wouldn't make a whole lot of sense if we didn't keep our eye on the goal.

Know Your Destination

I think you can see where I'm going with this.

If you don't know where you're going, you're never going to get there. It can be frighteningly easy to get side-tracked.

If you don't have goals, you're not going to get anywhere. Goals themselves may be one of those real big things but thoroughly thinking through what those goals really are for you... well, that's one of the most common "small things" that way too many business people simply seem to neglect. Nothing in the great game makes any sense until the goal gets established.

Obvious? Yeah, in theory, certainly.

In practice, however, it's always surprising to me how many businesses seem to lose track of where they're headed, of what they set out to do. That's basic, and that has to be the first consideration.

But goals have to be strategic in nature. When you first establish that goal, you may not know how you're going to get there. Don't sweat it. The key is to first know what you want to achieve. Make it as clear as a bell in your head. What are you in business for? What will your business look like if and when you succeed?

Then, once you've got that all-encompassing goal fixed firmly, begin the journey, knowing full well there may be a thousand different routes that could get you there.

As I've told you, my business was the fresh flower business. I set a goal to increase my sales volume—that is, my fresh flower customer base—by twenty percent every year. Although all kinds of ideas were always swirling around in my head at the time, in the beginning we were a very small business, and I really didn't know exactly how I was going to achieve the kind of growth I was targeting. But you know what? Just cementing those targets in my mind got me focusing on identifying the objectives that I needed to complete in order to hit my goals.

That's when I began looking at concrete objectives.

Goals are strategic. The objectives, then, are the multiple points along the way, the stepping stones on the journey, that are eventually going to get me there.

Goals don't necessarily need date limits, but objectives do. They need reasonable target dates. The business simply has to create that pressure in order to actually accomplish an objective.

In fact, it is critically important to prepare the equivalent of an assignment sheet for each specific objective. Who will do what by when? And, if that seems just way too small a thing to you, then please take my advice that that is one of those small things that will constantly amaze you with its ability to take you smoothly toward the big things. Most of the big stuff, the great game, is really played most successfully on some very small fields of battle.

And you know what definite, clear objectives will require of you? They'll require, along with intelligent scrutiny, a bit of common sense as well. Because goals can't be some lofty thing that makes it impossible for you to define what tasks you'll take to achieve the stepping stone objectives.

I mean, maybe you've come up with a goal to become the greatest person the world has ever known. Hmmm. Okay, uh, … good luck with that one, because you're going to need it. Not only are you up against Buddha and Alexander the Great and Abraham Lincoln, and …Jesus, for cryin' out loud, but good luck trying to lay out some concrete objectives for yourself! Where do you begin???

For me, it helps to identify real people who were successful, and to get to know them. I always enjoy reading their biographies. For example, Tom Monaghan, the founder of Dominos Pizza, has a pretty good one called *Pizza Tiger.* Ray Kroc of McDonalds and Jack Welch of General Electric also have great books.

I was lucky enough to know a few very successful men personally, the most notable being Stan Kresge, the son of the founder of Kmart, Sebastian Sperik Kresge. Stan was a member of the Detroit Rotary club back in the 70s and, when I found that out, I joined the Detroit Rotary Club. After a few weeks, I sat with him during a lunch and, what I found attracted me to him personally was the way his generosity seemed to exude from every aspect of his personality. That, to me, was the mark of a great man first and foremost; and secondly, although not any less impressive, was his remarkable success as an entrepreneur. As it happened, he also belonged to the Freemasons, of which I was a member, and this gave us a little bit of commonality to share. I never imposed myself on him, and only sat at his table occasionally, but I always got a nod and a kind word when I saw him.

There were many men like that with whom I intentionally crossed paths. Some only owned a tire store or two. They were playing the great game as well, albeit maybe in a slightly smaller arena.

But the point here is that you've got to be able to identify a goal, one that you can visualize and say, "Yes! If they can do it, so can I!"

Then you need to break that big, majestic goal down and develop shorter-term goals. Turn the big things into the small beginnings that can, in fact, be tackled. Once you've got those goals, you then must identify the objectives you're going to need to master in order to obtain those short-term goals, the ones that will eventually turn into life goals.

Maybe an example from my own life will help illustrate the point.

When I was still pretty young—late teens, I think—I was involved in a Masonic Youth Group called Demolay. I'd say that's about the first time I was exposed to any kind of actual "tool" for management. It was a good lesson, and one that stuck with me.

I was given the responsibility to run the Charity Committee for the entire state of Michigan. This involved about seventy local chapters, and roughly 7,000 members. I won't go into how it was that I was selected for this office, but maybe it'll be enough to just say that I had performed successfully in some earlier activities with the group.

At any rate, the tool I was given was a simple, but surprisingly powerful sheet that had the words "ASSIGNMENT SHEET" written right at the top. Then it stated the specific goals that I was to achieve. The GOALS were clear, and beneath them was a list of vague OBJECTIVES, with Target Dates. It was up to me to organize and execute the tactical means to achieve the objectives, and subsequently to reach the overall goals.

I have to admit, at first it seemed kind of daunting. But it didn't take very long for me, even as an authority-skeptical teenager, to see the clarity it afforded. The way I looked at it, I was empowered to take charge and execute my own plan as long as it obtained the objectives that would ultimately reach the GOALS as outlined. With so many people working together, and working on so many related facets of the one goal, I soon could see the necessity, the wisdom, of using the goal and target sheets to keep everyone informed, everyone clearly focused on the main end goal, as well as on each of the stepping-stone objectives we were joined together to try to achieve. Everyone knew from the start what their responsibilities were.

I could see that it probably didn't take a whole lot of time to put that Assignment Sheet together. A small beginning, right? But it was a real eye-opener mapping the path of what each of us was to do, and why we were doing it. Everyone was clear as could be about where we were all heading, what was our end goal. And that was a _BIG_ thing!

Any assignment given to someone ought to demonstrate the path to the goal. That is, it ought to spell out very clearly how the task they are being asked to take on will fit into the group's pursuit of a specific goal. There should be no question as to **_why_** they are being asked to achieve their assignment, about how their possibly small contribution will move all of us forward toward the big goal.

Target Dates

Allow me to emphasize the critical importance of putting target dates on objectives that will lead us to our goal. A goal without a specific target date is, unfortunately, not much more than a lofty wish. When an objective gets a target date, only then does it become real.

Did you ever wonder why students cram for exams, or put in all-nighters to get a term paper done? They had all semester, right? Yeah, but it's the imminent target date that all of a sudden gives us the required kick-in-the-butt to get that "goal" finally accomplished.

If there never was an exam, I'd imagine more than a few students wouldn't spend a whole lot of time studying that particular material. In the same way, if there was no required deadline for submission of a term paper, I'd imagine quite of few of them would never get written. In fact, I have an acquaintance who never quite got his Bachelor's Degree just because he still hasn't completed his final paper for one last course he took. That was about thirty years ago. But I'm sure he's almost done. Almost. Doesn't really matter; there was no specific due date. His prof told him he could hand it in whenever he completed it, and then she'd be happy to give him his grade. Hmmm, makes me wonder if that prof is still alive to fulfill that promise, should the need arise.

So, target dates are mighty important.

But, what if you don't accomplish the assigned task by the target date? What if some unseen obstacle gets in the way, causing you a largely unpredictable delay? Does it really make sense to abandon an objective because you missed the date?

Of course not! Stuff happens, right?

But here's the rub. If you do decide to change a target date, you'd better be growling at yourself as you do it. You'd better be angry as hell that you didn't foresee whatever obstacle was thrown across your path that you just didn't see coming! Who's to say that's not going to happen again? Who's to say that, if you've been blindsided once, you won't be blindsided again? I mean, the fair assumption here is that you knew what you were doing when you set that target date! You did, right? You had looked at the potential hurdles, you analyzed very carefully what it was going to take for your team to reach that finish line, and so you laid out a specific target date for its achievement.

Or, is it possible that, in fact, you did _not_ do some of those "small" things? Could that seemingly minor omission of just one person be what's holding up the whole train?

At the outset, take a closer look. If your target date is simply unrealistic; if it denies your team the necessary time to tackle whatever obstacles they're going to encounter, then you're going to have an awfully tough time motivating them to keep working at something, when the prospect of failure looms so doggone close, simply for lack of sufficient time.

On the other hand, if your target date is so loose, so lacking in any significant time pressure, then, unless your team is working on a completely unrelated-to-the-business experimental venture, whose success is questionable and nobody cares anyway, then there's a good chance your team will never complete their work. They might as well be doing a term paper…with no due date. When it comes to human beings, nothing in business gets done without a due date. If your team doesn't take your target dates as seriously as you do; if they aren't convinced of the importance of hitting those dates so that the overall target date of the larger goal can be achieved as needed, then you'll have a serious problem on your hands. It will likely be YOUR team that will hold up everyone else. I wonder who will pay the piper for that one.

Now, granted, if a project does get completed within the time constraint given, it may not be done perfectly! Don't sweat that so much! The perfection can always be added inside of a future time constraint. Besides, you may not have even recognized what it will take to move from excellence to perfection until you have first achieved the project. First, get it done!

You can always make improvements. In fact, with most products or services, the final improvements, the ones that move a good product or service from excellence to some measure of perfection, are the improvements that are implemented only after the product or service has been put into use. Is it any wonder that so many seemingly minor details in auto manufacturing end up being subjected to recalls? Is it really any wonder that we're not all driving black Ford Model T's any more? They got it done, but then they made some improvements.

Set a target date, and get it done. And then be sure to take a whole lot of pride in that achievement alone.

Therefore, if you absolutely *have to* change the dates, well then, change the dates. But you'd better do it grudgingly, and you'd better be growling at yourself as you do. Remember, those "small" things …are big.

Along with target dates, it's critical to have mile markers along the way to your goal as well. If you can't identify these, then you may have an awfully difficult time accomplishing any goal. Once you set your first objective, and of course give it its target date for achievement, then it's important to continue. Set the second objective and its own target date. And then set the third, and the fourth, and so on. Yes, of course, you CAN alter these as you mark your actual progress with each objective. But, if you do, you'd better be clenching your fists, and start the growling.

Bumps in the Road

Now here's the other side of that same coin.

You set your goals. You establish your stepping-stone objectives, and you give each objective well-thought-out target dates for achievement. But, despite your best efforts, things occasionally do NOT go as anticipated. Occasionally? Hmph, it happens a lot, doesn't it?

This is where you've got to be intelligently flexible.

I have an acquaintance who, in league with his wife, really wanted to increase the square footage of their home. They loved the location, the neighbors, the yard, but they just needed a whole lot more space for the kids, who apparently were growing taller than they'd expected. Anyway, they drew up plans to move the front walls of the house about fifteen feet more out towards the front. Major project, right? They're pretty handy people, as you may have guessed. But when they took their plans to the City Planners, they were told that that would put the front of their house illegally close to the street per the zoning code for that particular neighborhood.

I found myself smiling when he told me about this because he didn't even seem angry. No bitterness, no bellyaching, nothing! I was impressed.

When I asked him what he planned to do then, he immediately told me that he and his wife had simply altered their plan to instead increase their square footage by adding a second story to their house. Now that was flexible.

Here's the lesson.

If you find, after tackling a specific objective, that it turns out to be simply impractical—or maybe even illegal—then that's the time to be flexible in your objective. You're not altering the overall goal, of course, but you may have to reconsider your objectives and/or your target dates for them. I wonder how many times NASA had to do that before they finally achieved the goal of landing on the moon. Just a thought.

The bottom line to all of this discussion about goals and objectives is, above all, that you can't just ***HOPE*** that things are going to unfold as you want them to, by accident. C'mon! Has that happened to you a lot already? Yeah, me either. Set your goals, set your objectives, set your target dates, and get to work in an organized, methodical, readily-measurable manner. Get out there and get those small beginnings done—on time—so you can be assured of reaching the big things in the great game you're playing.

The End Point

While we're at it, do you know what the scariest thing in the military is? They say it's a second lieutenant with a compass. I guess you'd have to have had the experience of traipsing around in the woods with one to know that. The problem is, he isn't looking at the compass because he *knows* where he *is*. He's looking at that compass because he's wondering where the devil he's *going*! If you've ever tried it, you'll know that land navigating isn't the simplest thing to do! And, if it's a second lieutenant doing it, chances are pretty good that it's close to his first time navigating.

I have some delightful senior friends who love to explore on their road trips. He drives, and she navigates. But she navigates using a special map of the US that she found that has everything printed upside down so she can more easily follow it when they head south. As they say, many times they really don't know where they'll end up, but they do enjoy the journey even so. I'm sure that works for them. They have a lot of fun together. But may I remind you, reader, that that is a pretty lousy method with which to conduct a business. If you don't clearly know where you're heading, then I'm gonna bet that you're never going to get there.

Before I wrap up our discussion of goals, though, allow me to add one more thought.

No Destination Is Too Far

No goal is too lofty. None. As I've already mentioned, in this country anyway, you've got a good shot at being or doing pretty much whatever you want to be or to do—as long as you're willing to do the work necessary to achieve that goal.

But you've got to know, too, that it's going to be a lot easier to achieve any goal, but especially a particularly lofty one, if you can break it down to smaller, bite-size chunks.

How do you eat an elephant? One piece at a time.

Alright, alright. That may not be one of your lofty goals.

But I'm guessing you're reading this book because you do have the appreciably lofty goal of building a successful business. And to do so, you've got to have a goal, and a solid business plan of objectives and target dates to get you to that goal. But, as you set about determining your goal, keep your mind *open*. Keep it open to all the possibilities.

If you're fifty years old, for instance, and you really want to get into the medical field, there's a possibility that you won't be admitted to a formal medical school. You may not be able to actually become a doctor, starting at that age.

Okay, then there's a good reason to open your mind to near possibilities. First, identify what you, in fact, *can* do.

Evaluate the market conditions for that service. Find out what is doable for someone like you. Find out where there may be a need that you yourself can supply. And then set your goal, and begin taking your first steps toward that goal. Start doing one small thing after the other.

But be careful too. If you make your goal too finite, you may end up locking yourself in. Many people seem to identify too soon what they THINK their goal should be, and then they force their research only to fit that goal.

If you decide you want to become a doctor, even though you're fifty years old, you'll necessarily restrict yourself to researching medical schools that might admit a student like you into their program. Maybe your research will even take you to schools outside of this country!

But instead, maybe give some thought to *why* you want to become a doctor. Perhaps what you really want is to work with patients in a medical facility. Maybe you have had someone in your family helped in some amazing way by a doctor, and you'd like to emulate that.

But think about it carefully. What is your actual goal in seeking to be a doctor? What is it that you *really want to do*? What is your "why?" Because there's a real possibility that, while there may not be a ready avenue for you to become a doctor, there may be plenty of alternative avenues for you, even at your age, to do much of what you want to do professionally along those same lines, without having to actually be a doctor.

Open your mind to as many possibilities as you can. Keep your goal, especially at the outset, as broad as possible so that you can remain open to other avenues to achieve it.

The Strategy of the Trip

Always remember too that goals, by definition, are strategic. It's the tactics that are the practical steps taken to achieve the strategic goal. And sometimes the tactic might seem out of kilter with a goal. But it may well conform to the overall strategy of the goal.

For example, during WWII, the Allied Powers put a concerted effort into bombing Germany's ball bearing factories.

On the surface, of course, that might seem a little odd. There were no German soldiers in the ball bearing factories! To the Allied soldiers on the battlefield, I'd imagine they'd have preferred that the Allied bombers would have bombed instead the soldiers and tanks and what-not-else that were shooting at them! At the same time, anyone could see that taking out the ball bearing factories would soon cripple all the tanks and trucks and ships and planes and all kinds of other machinery that the Germans threw so heavily against the Allied armies. And, eventually, there would be no more functioning machinery left for the Germans to throw against anybody.

It's the overriding strategy that gives worth to the specific tactics. If the tactics do not fit beneath the overall umbrella of the strategy, then they really have no place in that venture. At the same time, without tactics, even the best strategies are absolutely worthless. It's pretty ineffective to have one without the other.

I play chess a little. I know enough to recognize the value of controlling the center squares on the board. I also know that sometimes I've got to sacrifice a piece or two in order to effect that objective. It might look like a bad move on the surface of it, but it often is a necessary support to the overall strategy of controlling the center of the board to win the game.

Here's another one from my own business playbook.

I had my share of obstacles and challenges in the flower business, and it wasn't long before I came to know that I was going to need to improve my ability to think creatively, to maybe tune up the old brain neurons to peak performance if I was ever going to be successful overcoming some of these challenges.

There are a number of effective ways, I knew, that people use to improve their mental faculties, creativity and others. Some people juggle, some meditate, others take long walks. I took a little different route.

I hired a German tutor, a fellow whom I paid to teach me to speak German. I didn't really have a seriously committed intention of actually learning the language. What I was immensely interested in, though, was the effort it was going to take my brain to think in a way I'd never thought before. I knew that learning a language— or at least making a serious attempt to learn one—was going to sharpen up the gray matter. And it did. It most certainly did.

I never did learn to speak German all that well. In fact, I doubt I could get from the airport to the hotel in Berlin. However, I did learn enough to translate a bit of the highly-regarded 19th-century Prussian Lieutenant General Gerhard von Scharnhorst (1755-1813) of Napoleonic Wars fame:

I have perceived that man, with courage and will power, can overcome everything.

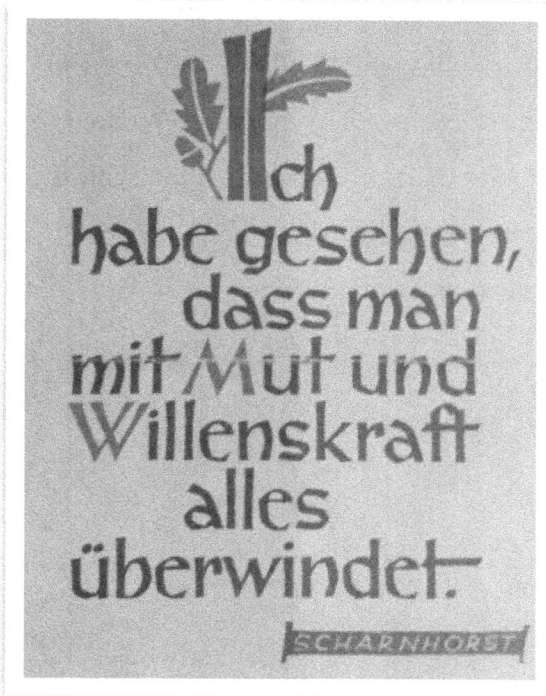

I always liked Scharnhorst, as he was the tutor to Von Clausewitz, the famous Prussian who wrote *On War*, a brilliant book on military theory.

That said...I'd have trouble ordering a beer in Munich.

But you know what? I could almost immediately see the improvement in both my ability to concentrate on a problem, and to seek out reasonably innovative solutions to them. It was kind of a strange <u>tactic</u>, I suppose, but it fit my <u>strategy</u> wonderfully. Small thing, but a sweet result!

At this point, I think I can guess what you're thinking. How did I ever find the time to study a foreign language when I'm hustling to juggle all the demands of a large business?

Well, maybe I can help. We're talking about time management now too, and, just like setting goals, objectives, and target dates, time management is absolutely essential. Without good time management, you will just become a fireman. You'll be putting out fires one after the other. Let's move on to a discussion of that right now. I think we've got time.

Chapter 5—Time: Friend or Foe?

Time: is it your friend or foe? It surely can be either.

If you lose a little money in your business…well, you can replace it eventually. If you lose good personnel, that's often a little tougher to replace, isn't it? But, in fact, that too is doable. You can lose product also, of course. Believe me, I know. My business was fresh flowers. And flowers don't stay fresh forever.

But the one thing you can't ever replace is time.

I can assure you from a wealth of experience that managing your time is just about the biggest "small" thing you can do, on a daily basis at least, that will streamline your trip to that lofty goal you've set for yourself and your company. When you play in the great game, everyone plays on the same playing field, and everyone has to play by the same game clock.

You've only got so much of it, just like everybody else.

So you've got tons of stuff to get done, just as do your competitors. And very often what success comes down to is you using your time a little better than your competition. You might have better product. You could have better people too. But you both have the exact same amount of time. So if you want to give yourself a powerful edge, learn to manage your time.

I'm talking about managing your hours, your days, your weeks, your months, and then your years, one after the other. Don't let them get away from you. You never get them back.

What's the consequence of poor time management? It is that you will inevitably end up spending all of your time trying to handle situations—problems by now—that have become urgent. You will simply not have the time to do what really needs to be done by you, which is to handle plans and activities that are the most important to the company's progress forward…before they ever get "urgent."

Every objective, every individual activity, requires a date, or a time, or maybe even a season. In the flower business, at least a season.

Once an activity slips past its planned deadline for completion, it is likely going to quickly become urgent. You're going to have to drop whatever you're doing just to handle this issue. The solution, of course, is to recognize the importance of planning ahead, for whatever. Do the *small* things right at the beginning!

I have always found it helpful, for example, to set aside separate tasks for separate days and times. Maybe I'll focus on finance on Monday mornings, personnel issues on Tuesday mornings, maybe our ad campaigns on Wednesday mornings, with a special focus on our Social Media on Thursdays. Fridays can be a little flexible because I've tackled the key issues on the previous days of the week. I also used to try to leave at least a certain portion of my afternoons for conferences with staff, or for spending a little extra time focusing on the resolution of a particularly troublesome challenge, or else to focus on open-minded creative thinking with a team of outside and in-company consultants.

Whatever your own method, be sure to take control of your own schedule. If you don't, I can guarantee that it will rapidly and unsympathetically take control of you.

And this certainly applies to just about any project, whether in business or elsewhere. If you're running a political campaign, heaven forbid, you can make the calendar and the clock work for you, or you can allow them to grow into monsters that will most certainly keep you from getting a good night's sleep.

Even at home, you could fairly simply assign Mondays as your "wash day," Tuesdays as market day, and so on.

Whatever you're taking on, see if you can block out the required separate tasks, give them their respective target dates, and do everything in your power to stick to the schedule as you've planned it. As you well know, *LIFE* is a pretty great game too.

Time management is your key to being able to focus on what is important for your business. You've got to be able to focus. Your company needs you to be able to focus. If you can't get control of your time, however, you will find yourself trying to handle so many interruptions, side tracks, and what-not else, probably primarily because, since they weren't handled properly in the steady planning process, they have now become urgent. And you will be able to focus on nothing else, at least for that time being.

Did I mention what frustration does to your focus? Hmph, I probably don't have to.

And, speaking of frustration, maybe consider this: I always try to divide my day into three equal parts: 1) my vocation—that is, my business; 2) helping others, or activities unrelated to my business; and 3) rest and refreshment. Sometimes it's pretty challenging, I'll admit. But I'll also say that it is in this way that I've been able to keep my head on straight. It's how I've been able to conduct a pretty complex business without experiencing the dreaded "burn out." If you're over-working yourself, and putting in hour after hour with your business that you just don't have, it's going to take a toll on everything else in your life. Your family is going to suffer, your spouse is going to suffer, and you too will certainly suffer, not least of all your very bodily and mental health.

Make time your friend, and it will help pave the road to success like few other elements can.

Chapter 6– $60 Thousand Dollars to $750 Million Dollars?

You've been patient, reader, and I much appreciate it. Up to this point, we've discussed some of the very basic principles behind running a successful business. I've made several limited references to my own business, but I haven't yet put the whole story before you for your own evaluation.

Sure, my business was different from yours. But the principles underlying success in a business are well established. They allow for just about anyone who is willing to learn them and practice them to enjoy whatever level of success they might desire. My only purpose in telling you my own story is to demonstrate to you that I'm not anything special. I don't have any special business gifts. And, like most of us in business at the start, money—that is, investment capital—was certainly a big mean ogre in the road.

Even so, you're more than welcome to skip over this chapter. In truth, I wouldn't blame you. I've had the good fortune to have been very successful in my business, so it would be pretty easy for you to think that it was a piece of cake for me. Believe me, in the telling of this, as you'll see, I most certainly do not mean to imply any boast whatsoever. In fact, I think you'll see that what I did is something that anybody could do.

There's no question that my journey had its obstacles, and I fell on my face plenty of times. I'm kinda surprised my nose isn't flatter. But if my story of diligent perseverance, with a touch of creative problem-solving, with my working hard to develop relationships with others who could help me…if all of that might be of some help to you in your own journey, well then, I hope you'll find my story worthwhile, and primarily in your own interest.

I must tell you, I absolutely LOVE playing the great game! I'm pretty good at it now, and that goes a long way toward my loving to play. But let me assure you that I am sincerely anxious for you to love it as much as I do. I've written this book primarily to help you enjoy the same passion, and the same success, that I have enjoyed. And, as you'll see here, the BIG things—the successes—all start with some very small beginnings. Maybe we can take a look at a few of those beginnings now, and I think you'll readily see what I mean. Business success is much more a matter of diligent, intelligent work than it is anything of raw luck, as I believe you'll see. And that means it's available to anyone.

My Small Beginnings

I read a lot. And I have a pretty positive outlook on things. I don't mean only now, but I seem to have always had that, ever since I can remember back in high school.

I used to work for my father and mother back then in the flower shop that they owned.

Here are my parents, Florence and Wesley Berry, Sr., at their 50th Wedding Anniversary party in 1995, shortly after my father's retirement.

Working together with them brought our family—my two older sisters and me—a pretty comfortable life where, while maybe we didn't have everything our little hearts desired, we never wanted for anything important, lived in a nice house, we had clothes as nice as any of our classmates then, and we always had enough to eat. No complaints. My mother and father really loved their flower business, and did reasonably well with it. They had two stores: one in the City of Detroit ,and the other was in our own hometown of West Bloomfield, Michigan.

My parents always hoped, I suppose, that their flower business would evolve into a family business that at least one of their kids would step into and carry on. My sisters and I began to help out there as soon and as much as we were able, starting with a formal work schedule and hourly wage when we were yet in high school.

According to my father, the business always did fairly well, brought in roughly $60K/yr during my high school years. Mom and Dad really enjoyed it and took pride in what they had created and nurtured. In retrospect, I really applaud them for following a passion they had and making it work well enough to comfortably support a family.

Then came 1967.

Detroit erupted into the worst race riot in the city's history. Stores were torched, businesses broken into, and many neighborhoods took a severe hit, beginning a decline that far too many never really recovered from. Our Detroit store was not exempt. Nor was the surrounding neighborhood. And, obviously, our flower business in that Detroit store was terribly affected.

At that point in my life I was at a crossroads of sorts. Like anyone around seventeen or eighteen years of age, I was grappling with what I wanted to do with my life. I'd earlier attended a military school for my seventh through ninth grades, and a couple of summers after that. I'd grown to like and appreciate a lot of what I'd learned there. So naturally, going into the military as a career was something I'd begun to consider pretty seriously.

At about the same time, I found myself pondering a move to California to attend a university and possibly pursue a business career there, probably completely unrelated to the flower business. Then came two job offers: one in San Francisco, and the other all the way on the other side of the world in Sydney, Australia. Mighty appealing stuff for a young kid just starting out.

My two older sisters had already decided they'd pursue paths other than working with our parents, so that meant that my parents would have to find other employees to help with the business, but at a time when that business was beginning to suffer substantially. That wasn't only because of what had happened to our Detroit outlet.

Within just a few years after that, the entire country began to feel the pinch of OPEC's oil embargo. Flower delivery takes gasoline, so our overhead was climbing as it never had before. And our potential customers found themselves shelling out more and more cash just so their cars would get them to work every day. That didn't leave them anything with which to indulge in a relative non-necessity like flowers.

We were in a deep recession. This little business with four employees—that is, including my mom and dad—all of a sudden could not produce enough profit for my parents even to cash their own paychecks. Things did not look good. We ate a lot of baloney sandwiches.

And here I was debating my next step into the future.

As it happened then, one day my dad came to me and made a statement that literally changed my life. He said, "If you leave, Wes, chances are good that the business will no longer be here when you return."

If there was ever a time for calm, quiet, clear, meditative thinking, this was it.

There was no question in my mind that I really enjoyed the idea of a family business, and working alongside my own parents was an absolute delight. They're great people, and I wanted to be very much like them. The problem, of course, especially at that particular time in our business's history, was the money. Despite the recent setbacks, there continued to be just enough profit in it to get us by day to day. And my parents were confident that, with a little help from family, much more than outside employees, they could bring the business around to recover its former profitability.

But I wasn't so sure.

I guess I'd have to chalk it up to youth and crazy ambition as I look back at it now, but I was concerned that, when I had my own family someday, would there be enough in that business for two families? Would I be able to make it for a lot of years—until I could possibly afford to buy the business from my parents, and they could retire in the comfort earned. In the meantime, though, would I be able to make it, to raise my own family, on the salary of one of their employees?

It wasn't a very easy decision to make, I'm afraid. As I've said, I've always been a died-in-the-wool optimist, and I was never terribly adverse to taking risks. This was a life decision here. It was one that I knew I'd be spending at least the next five years or so of my young life, and hopefully the rest of my working life after that, to make it work. Those five years might end up just being wasted. I might fail and have to start from scratch with something else, something that would likely be unfamiliar to me.

After a lot of dinnertime discussion with my parents, and then a whole lot of talking with myself, and even after some hard-nosed conversations with the Big Man upstairs, I made the decision to go all-in with the family flower business. I'd have to say the primary reason was simply this: I seemed to have a passion for business, any business, and this was one business I already knew forward and backward. At the very least, I reasoned, that was going to give me a leg up.

At the same time, if I was going to get involved, I knew I'd have to find a way to make it even more profitable than it already was if it was to support both them and me; especially with my zany youthful ambitions of grandeur, hopes of traveling to see the world, hopes of being able to make significant financial and

personal contributions to so many causes that I thought would make this world a better place. Y'know, youthful ambitions, right?

I also had the advantage of being groomed for leadership both by military school and by my involvement with DeMolay. Yeah, that's me on the left in…ahem, full battle array but feeling mighty proud of the country I was preparing to serve in some fashion or other. I never doubted my ability to lead or to succeed in any task that I would undertake, and so I was concerned about getting myself involved in a business that simply did not have the innate capacity to permit that level of success.

So I started in. For my commitment, my parents gave me a ten percent stake in the business. At that point, to my mind, I became a business owner, and began to take on the expected work ethic of one. I worked long hours, tried to work as smart as I could, and did everything possible to serve our customers as efficiently and professionally as possible, even as I sought ways to increase our customer base. To illustrate our current discussion in this book, I can tell you, reader, that I started doing a whole lot of small things…beginnings, if you will. Alongside my mother and father, I also constantly sought ways to cut our overhead. My father, as it turned out, was big on that. He was big on cutting costs, but a little sheepish when it came to ways to increase income beyond all that we were already doing with our two stores.

It wasn't long before the obvious stood before me. I could see incremental growth in our income from our meager cost-cutting, a little more from all the extra hours I was putting in. But it was astoundingly clear to me that I was never going to be able to continue at this pace, or increase the hours I was already spending with the business to where the profits could come anywhere near what I was hoping for. There had to be another way.

So we talked, Dad and me. We talked a lot about what could be done to correct the course. For him, though, it remained all about how to cut costs and raise prices, which, granted, at a ground level sounds like a very reasonable approach. Most business consultants would, I dare say, suggest the same thing.

But, for various reasons, this just did not sit right with me. So, I began searching for ways to lower prices, lower costs, and increase volume. Over and over, only the lowering of costs seemed to take root with my dad.

In those days, of course, there was no internet. We used a thing called a library. So that's where I went, and began intensive research on marketing and advertising ideas. If I do anything well, I'd have to say it's research. I'd been a top-notch debater in high school, and you simply can't succeed in something like that without a heckuva lot of research capabilities. So I had them.

So…I'm helping to run a flower business…and I'm at the library reading… Small things, right? But this first step, of many small steps, was a critical beginning, and one that supported my overall goal of turning our business into a comfortably huge success for all of us.

After some measured study, I spoke with my parents again. I knew the workings of the business fairly well, of course, so I had put pencil to paper and started to rack my brain, I told them. After a little time, and a whole lot of recalculations, I had come up with a variety of workable plans to show them, which I then tried to convince them would increase our sales. We could do TV and radio spots, for one. We could open more storefront outlets perhaps. Maybe we could purchase our flowers from growers who had farms in South America, and thus cut out the middle man.

My father, always reasonably but not overly frugal, listened carefully to everything I said. I really appreciated that. I sorta knew they were both pretty content with where the business was, despite its temporary hard times. And I knew that they were sympathetic, and even encouraging, to my youthful excitement and ambitions. Given all that, though, I was still surprised when my father gave me his answer.

He sat back in his chair, took a deep breath, and thought about all that I had said long and hard. He then turned to me and actually gave me carte blanche to do whatever I thought I could do to make the business more profitable.

I was utterly amazed. It was all I could do to keep myself from jumping up from the table and going over to him and giving him a bear hug for the confidence he was showing in his son! And then he added one more small phrase: "As long," he said, "as it doesn't cost any money."

All of a sudden, I could hear the wind in my sails sorta being quietly ushered out the door.

It was Dad's opinion that, while the business did provide us with a decent living, it did not, however, provide enough surplus cash for any kind of improvements or investments into its own future. As he saw it, whatever we might be able to do, we'd have to do solely with our own labor, which meant either working harder —something I wasn't sure was even possible—or working smarter.

To be honest, though, I could certainly understand his position. But at the same time, I could also feel my frustration building. And, to tell you the truth, at this point, Sydney was starting to look like a pretty good idea.

As part of my research, of course, I'd read a couple of business books, as I'm sure all of us have. To a fault, all successful people spoke, in some manner or other, about the power of positive thinking, about turning lemons into lemonade, about searching hard for the positive in any negative. Remember how we just talked, in our last chapter, about keeping your mind open to alternative strategies when you come upon an oak tree lying across your road?

Yeah…well, that ain't so easy sometimes. I needed help, but I was clueless about where I might get it.

So I started searching for my answer in a different way. Open mind, right? I started to seek out the smartest and most successful persons in the room everywhere I went. I'd sit as close to them as possible and try to engage them in conversation. This happened in church, at trade events, club meetings, and anywhere else I could find them. However, I was not just talking with these people; I was learning all kinds of little and big things. But still no workable tips on how to get things jump-started without spending any money.

Now that I think back on it, I wish that Rhonda Byrne's book *The Secret* had come out by that time. It didn't, of course. Therefore, I didn't realize back then that, when we set our minds to achieve something, and then work our buns off to make it happen, somehow the planets line up to help us succeed. Things come across our path that, were we not focused on one thing in particular, we might never have even noticed, or certainly not taken advantage of. I didn't realize it then, but I was about to become just one more living proof of that.

Great book, by the way, *The Secret*! If you get a chance, give it a read-through. It's one of those things that can be a powerful life-changer. It will offer you a perspective, a way of thinking about this world—business and otherwise—that, while it doesn't seem to be the perspective *most* people see the world with, it is nonetheless the one that I've noticed most *successful* people do. Give it a shot.

Remember when I was telling you in chapter two about my involvement with my youth group, and how I was made the chairman of the Charity Committee? Remember my very first exposure to an Assignment Sheet, with target dates that I actually had to adhere to? Well, I had nothing to lose, and everything to gain if I could actually find some way to increase our business at the same time as I respected my father's requirement that we spend no more money. So I set a goal for myself to learn everything I could, to explore every possible way to improve a business …for free. There had to be something.

Remember that there was no internet back then. Makes you wonder how civilization survived, right? But we did have libraries. So that's where I went—again.

But, believe it or not, there isn't a whole lot of material written about how to increase your business without spending any money. Funny, no?

I was starting to get a little ticked. There had to be a way, but it sure wasn't crying out to me! This kind of stuff can be frustrating and depressing. It can rob you of a couple of good nights' sleep, and, if it gets out of control, it can ruin your life. If you're reading this book, I think you understand what I'm talking about. It's easy to tell someone to stay positive in the face of adversity, but it's not always easy to do it ourselves, y'know?

Anyway, I think this is where the ol' planets started to line up a little to give me a quick boost.

Meeting Leo

I have been active with the Masons for the better part of my life, even when I was still a teen. I think I was about seventeen when I attended a DeMolay workshop one day at which a very successful businessman—a Mason friend of my father, in fact— was the speaker. His name is Leo Harrawood. He had been a WWII veteran who was now in his mid-fifties, and he was one of the most dynamic, remarkable-in-every-way people I have ever had the great pleasure of meeting. He was there that day to give a

85

motivational presentation, and I was absolutely amazed at this man's energy, at the largeness of his very presence! Whoa.

He spoke about how, when he was wounded by multiple machine gun fire while landing on a beach in the Pacific, how this changed his life in a most dynamic and positive way. That alone was a show-stopper. The audience was mesmerized. Me too. His injuries were so severe, he told us, that if he did end up surviving, he was told that he could expect, at best, to remain severely crippled for the rest of his life. Then, as our jaws dropped just a little further, he went on to declare to us that this was actually one of the greatest gifts of his life. But it was a gift that few could understand.

As it happened, Leo did survive. But not only that, he walked again too, and without so much as a limp. In fact, he said the whole experience served to make him much stronger than he had been before it, but not only physically. With the help of a cherished Navy chaplain who guided his transformation, Leo began to change the very way he thought.

All it takes sometimes is someone like this stepping into our lives. If we're ready for it, it can certainly make all the difference. I'll tell you how in this instance.

One evening after that talk, while I was doing some paperwork in the Michigan DeMolay Office in the Detroit Masonic Temple, the same Leo Harrawood suddenly stopped in. And in short order he told me to meet him next Tuesday at 6:30 a.m. at a restaurant in Farmington Hills, the next town over from ours, for breakfast. At the time, I didn't realize this was a test of sorts.

As I look back at it now, getting to that breakfast on time was actually a pretty small beginning. But sometimes I wonder what my life would have looked like if I had shown up late that morning, because it turned out to be one of the biggest first steps I was to take on a long journey to a wonderfully successful life.

Anyway, so we talked. And he got to know me, although I quickly got the impression that he had done his homework on me before that breakfast. I was a little surprised, a little taken aback, I guess, when he remarked about a gunshot wound that I had recently received. But that was only the tip of the iceberg. He knew as well about my aspirations, my youthful ambitious tendencies, and of my desire to do something significant with my life.

As I write this now after all these years, I'll admit that my recollection of his exact words might be a little off. But the meaning of those words is certainly not. It is still clear as a bell to me. He told me that I am the master of my own life. Nobody else. I am the builder of who I will be. And I alone am responsible for everything that happens in my life. Whatever happens to me, it is I myself who attracts it to me. I myself.

Hmph, I guess you'd have to say he was ahead of his time, huh? I couldn't help but think of Leo's words when I first picked up *The Secret*. How right he was way back then.

He went on to say that every coin has two sides, and that everything in life is both positive and negative. I remember thinking, "Was he not absolute living proof of that?" What he meant was that it was up to me to find the good in everything that happens to me, just as he himself had done. By doing so, he told me, success in life was within the grasp of every individual without exception.

Then he spoke to me about the power of prayer.

Now I don't mean to get all pious on you, reader, but I've gotta tell you that, like most people, I do believe that there's a "higher power," "God," if you will. And I also believe He's heavily invested in each one of us. So my faith tells me that prayer is just one of the ways we can connect with Him. I do. And sometimes I feel like it's effective communication, and then other times I feel like I'm spinning my spiritual wheels, and nothing's getting communicated at all. I'm no theologian, and I'm certainly not any kind of religious guru. But when Leo started talking about it, somehow it was different. The whole concept of prayer and spirituality started to come alive in ways that I hadn't ever heard before. Another small beginning, right?

The long and short of what he told me, though, was that prayer does play a significant role in altering our subconscious mind to where our subconscious can actually charge and direct our conscious mind to obtain those lofty goals I had set for myself. That had been true for him, he told me, and it had been true for all kinds of people he had helped, especially in the world of business.

In fact, to make his point wholly memorable, he actually banged his hand on the table and said to me, with this stern, ultra-serious look on his face, "Set your goals and objectives, and establish target dates for each of them, and you WILL realize them! You've got to visualize your goals, even if you don't know right now how the devil you're ever going to accomplish them—and then let your mind lead the way."

He went a little further. "Take a small piece of paper," he said, "and write down whatever you would wish for, and keep that paper with you at all times. That paper is going to keep your subconscious riveted on that goal." He explained to me that this was a powerful tool, and that I ought to use it with deliberate caution. "Don't say, 'I want this job or that job.' Describe the qualities of the job or position you desire! Set your goals, let your subconscious take control, and the next thing you'll know, the necessary tasks will present themselves."

So I did. And I kept that piece of paper in my wallet…for years.

Leo was right. It works. Like magic it works. Such a seemingly simple technique, somehow connecting with the universe, as they say in *The Secret*, and the universe starts to bend to lend you a hand. I know, I know. Sounds a little bizarre, doesn't it? But believe me, I've met very few marvelously successful people who are not also familiar with this same principle acting in their own lives.

Today, I no longer need that little piece of paper. His words were right on the mark. I have accomplished every one of those goals that I wrote down that day. Please stick with me just a little longer, and I'll tell you how it all came about.

But that initial conversation with Leo covered a whole lot more ground than just that. He explained several other techniques like vision boards, and how to steer a conversation. We'll talk about those in a later chapter. He emphasized how positive thoughts would attract positive results, and why it is so important to always frame your thoughts in a positive context. He talked about the importance of associating with the kind of person I myself would wish to emulate; something about how birds of a feather flock together. At least I got that one without too much headwork. He also spoke to me about the whole "dress for success" thing, and about how basics like good manners make the man. And you know what? He was especially keen on forgiving yourself when you get off track. His remedy? "Just hop back on that track and begin again that positive way of thinking as quickly as you can!"

Because of his amazing success in business and in life, his wonderful ability to speak about it with such enthusiasm, and his ever-ready willingness to share what he had learned with anyone who cared to listen, Leo Harrawood was a man in great demand. Although I rarely had the opportunity to talk with him again after that eye-opening morning, I did see him many times about the town. He'd give me a glance and a nod, and I knew what he expected. I'd see him in crowded rooms, sometimes I'd see him just driving or walking, and one time he was even cutting the grass in front of a very large building that I later learned he owned. I smile to myself when I think that he almost seemed to haunt me!

But, if so, he "haunted" me in the very best of ways, as his words have lingered in my mind for all these many years since.

And here's the rub. As I think about it, it seems to me that most of what Leo told me that morning was stuff that I had already heard, from my father, from my grandfather, and even in Sunday school. But somehow when he banged that table, the impact of his words—the same words maybe that I had heard before—those

words penetrated into spaces in me that I don't think I ever even knew existed. That's Leo in the photo; one of my very special personal mentors and heroes.

I was learning those same concepts, but in a whole different way. And he had a real knack for putting all of it together in a way that enabled me to see how it could all play out in my own life and career. That conversation was the first day of *my* beginning to understand the importance of small beginnings, which put me on a pathway to great big things. I guess another way to say it is that Leo that day provided me with some very simple, yet amazingly powerful tools. Over the years, I have availed myself of that toolbox he gave me, and have even added a few new tools of my own. But first and foremost, to my mind, is the power of positive thinking. It has the ability to accomplish most anything; and it constantly reminds me that "good" can be found in the very darkest corners of life's travels.

As I think about it here now as I write, I'm struck by how my own father often taught much the same. He used to tell us that he had a favorite Bible verse: "Ask and it will be given to you; seek and you will find; knock and the door will be opened to you." (Mt 7:7). As an adult, I can easily acknowledge now that my father was essentially saying what Leo had said to me. But I have to admit that it took a while for the idea behind it to sink into my head; the idea that this was required for your inner dialogue as well as for your worldly engagements. That was the twist. In fact, I remember discussing this same verse with my childhood minister, Pastor Freed, who told me that I should read *all* of Matthew Chapter 7, and that there was much more there for me to learn. Pastors. Don't ya just love 'em!

But let me continue with the story I began to tell you.

A New Idea

I was telling you how my father had given me a ten percent stake in his business, and had allowed me to do whatever I thought would improve our business…as long as it didn't cost any money. That's a fairly hefty challenge in anybody's book.

Alright, so my options were to get upset, maybe to decide that the goal was impossible, and throw in the towel. But I couldn't help but remember what Leo had hammered home to me about always looking for the positive in anything that at first appears to be negative. So I spent a lot of time thinking, trying to focus on the challenge. It occurred to me that this can't be the first time this problem was faced by people in business. There must be others out there who have tackled this, and have come out successful.

So I was at a business conference one day, still focusing on my father's challenge, and there was a man there whom had achieved a very high level of success in his own business. I took a couple of deep breaths, hustled a little, wormed my way around some, and finally worked it out so I was sitting at the dinner table right next to him.

Be assured that it made me nervous to be sitting there. I mean, who was I, after all?

But I sometimes wonder now where I'd be today if I had not mustered up the courage, the fake confidence, to just go ahead and risk sitting next to this man. He was a man whom many others probably would have liked to join in conversations with themselves. Another small, albeit mildly courageous beginning, right?

After the usual small talk, I put my question to him, something like, "Our business needs to grow substantially, but it doesn't have any capital to do that." As I think about it today, even that, particularly at a business conference, was a pretty bold admission. It was embarrassing to admit to any other business owner that your business wasn't making money. It did make me a little nervous to tell him that. But at the same time I felt like I was up against a rock and a hard place, had exhausted what resources I had been able to consult about this, had come up with nothing worthwhile, and so I had to take the risk. I knew full well that there was a strong possibility this man might simply mock me, write me off as an amateur, and maybe even let other business owners know that we weren't really doing all that well. So, yeah, I was nervous.

But I had to ask. Just maybe he'd be able to offer me something that could move me forward.

So I continued. "Can you say what is the most beneficial thing you've done for your business that didn't cost you any money?"

I braced myself for the laughter.

But it never came. In fact, I watched him as he thought it over. To be sure, he hemmed and hawed a bit as he talked about the importance of securing financing, etc. But I was patient. And I think he recognized that my question was serious.

So eventually he told me something that gave me a possible tool to begin to move a mountain. He leaned into me, and said simply, "Trade."

Then he went on to tell me how he had benefited from barter and, while it wasn't exactly void of cost for his company, it did allow him to do things he simply would not otherwise have been able to do. More specifically, he said that TV and radio stations garner their income from broadcasting ads for businesses. Of course. But many times they simply don't fill up all of their available time slots. Therefore, it's possible once in a while to take those "remnants," as they called them, or, in their jargon, ROS (Run of Station) spots, in a trade by exchanging something that your company has that the owners or program managers of the stations can use. He suggested, if I wanted to try this out, that I ought to call all of the local stations and let them know Wesley Berry Flowers would like to be considered for any of these spots that might become available, and that we could offer them such-

and-such in exchange. He suggested I call them on the first of the
month—every single month.

I wasn't sure, but it was something. I could feel my
tarnished heart beginning to beat just a little bit stronger. I guess
that's what hope can do for you. Finally, I'd been given a possible
path. It was admittedly a pretty small one on the surface, that is, a
small beginning. But, lo and behold, it really wouldn't cost too
much money.

I had no place else to turn. I had to give it a try.

So that's what I began to do. It did take time, of course, but
it didn't cost any money. I called every single TV and radio station
in the whole Detroit Metropolitan area. Most of them were polite,
to be sure, but I could also tell that my call wasn't their most
exciting call every month.

"Uh, what's your name again?"

"And what does your company do?"

"Oh, you again. What was it you wanted again?"

"Didn't you call us last month, and we told you we didn't
have anything? Yeah, well, maybe call next month; we'll see."

Even though I wasn't particularly enthusiastic about
spending a day or two at the beginning of every month calling
these same stations, and hearing these same "no's," I did my very

best to keep my energy up as I called. I was friendly, respectful, enthusiastic. As I saw it, I was not only trying to get a sale, but more importantly, I was trying to get a new business relationship off the ground. I only needed one positive response, one small spot on any radio station at all, and I knew that would buoy my spirits up. Besides, it might be the start of a small upsurge in sales of flowers. I mean, ultimately, wasn't that the point?

After a few months, I was surprised when a few of the program managers I had been calling every month began addressing me as Wes. Many of them stopped asking who I was, or, "What was your company, again?" To me, at this point, that was a victory. That was progress! And I was willing to take any positive progress I could muster. I suppose, when you're trying to get those infernal planets to line up in your favor for a change, you've got to take whatever you can get. More small beginnings.

Once again, as I write this, I find myself wondering what might have happened if I'd grown discouraged, especially after months and months of these unnerving "cold calls" without a single anything to call a success, or at least something small to keep me doing it. But nothing. Or at least nothing that brought us any extra sales. And I must admit that, when month-after-month came to its final days, I found myself dreading having to spend probably another day or two at the start of the coming month, possibly wasting an awful lot of apparently unproductive time, calling these same station managers, or whomever would talk to me, in an attempt to essentially get something for free. But I kept my Leo Harrawood paper in my pocket; remember, the one with my goals written down on it? And that at least got me straightening out my attitude, putting a smile on my face, and a positive spin in my phone voice. And come the first of the month, I started again making the calls all over again.

Finally, after fully six months, I had a station manager pick up the phone, hear my voice, and answer half-excitedly with, "Wes Berry, I was just going to call you!"

I could feel my heart skip a beat.

"Sure, what can I do for you?" I said.

"Look, Wes, we're having an end-of-the-year banquet for our large sales staff in a few weeks, and I was wondering if you could supply us with a boatload of corsages that we could give out to all of the women who are working for us here."

I was flabbergasted. On the inside, of course. But I impressed myself with how calm I was able to act as I spoke. "Sure thing! How many do you think you'll need, and when do you need them by? And thanks!"

That was the first deal. It actually got us a fairly substantial amount of air time, and I was delighted at how even that little bit ramped up our business for a brief time.

As it turns out, radio and TV stations invite their corporate advertisers into the station for a whole variety of reasons, and most of those occasions seem to go over a lot more smoothly for them when there are beautiful arrangements of flowers at the dinner tables while the station makes its presentations. It turns out too that employees seem to feel better about their office environment when there is an abundance of live plants all around them. And heaven knows it's always better when you have a business associate, perhaps someone like Wesley Berry Flowers, to stop in on a regular basis to make sure those plants stay healthy and beautiful.

So I began to frequent this station.

But I also made sure to take the time to stop in and say "hi" to that same station manager, and to anyone else I'd stumble upon there. People like to buy from people they know and like, right? Any and every business book told me that! So I made a diplomatic effort to get to know them, their business, and for them to get to know me. And I made sure they got some of our most beautiful flowers and arrangements, and that they got them when they needed them. I made sure they became well aware that we were reliable. They could trust us to get the job done for them. And I always did whatever I could to make sure that they loved working with us.

Yeah, that took a little more time out of my day, it's true. But I saw it as one of those small beginnings. I knew where this could eventually lead us.

Well, this one little success kept me motivated to continue my monthly calls to the other stations. And, you know what? It seems that radio and TV station managers go to business conferences with other station managers and they talk together. Go figure, eh? And they share what they're doing with each other too, even down to where they get their plants and fancy corsages. Isn't that something?

In time I began to frequent a few more stations, and Wesley Berry Flowers started popping up on radio and TV ads all over the metro area—on trade. In a remarkably short time, we found ourselves advertising on classic rock stations, hard rock stations, talk stations, minority stations, and everything else under the sun. Sometimes when we'd run a special, say, on roses at Valentine's Day. We could tell by the crowds lining up outside (yeah, I know ...*crowds*!) what radio station they'd heard the ad on! Believe it or not, punk rockers dress a lot differently than people who listen to business talk radio. Amazing, right?

But you know what's even more amazing? When I first started calling radio and TV stations, Wesley Berry Flowers was working at a pace of about $60K/yr. About six months after I had my first corsage success, we had bumped up to a pace of $500K/yr. I was getting ready to ask my father if I could spend a little money now.

So how did that come about?

Well, as you might suspect by now, it started with rather small beginnings. I showed up on time. I made sure to provide a quality product coupled with my quality service. I worked at developing as many positive personal business relationships as I could that I knew would advance our business.

Small beginnings, right? But at this point the great game was becoming exceptionally exciting to play. I could soon see that these small beginnings had a pretty doggone good potential to lead us to some mighty big things. And they did.

From Radio to Television

The next thing I knew, we were involved in the designing of the sets for several television shows and soon ended up providing extensive plants and floral arrangements for the shows on a daily basis. This alone earned us a ten-second credit on each of these shows, some of which I chose to use right away on that very show, others of which I chose to save and accumulate for later use. These seemingly "small beginnings," by the way, when clustered together and used during our peak seasons—Valentine's Day, Mother's Day, Christmas, etc.—turned out to be the beginning of some very big things for us.

Pretty soon we found ourselves in a position to advertise on every major television and radio station in the metro area just because of these very small ten-second beginnings. And, following shortly after that increased exposure, we began getting involved in numerous radio show promotions and giveaways as well.

To my surprise and delight, I soon found myself a guest on several of these same radio and television shows, being interviewed about all sorts of things, although ostensibly about the nature of my business.

Prompted then by these new media successes, I began to send out various news releases, and that in turn led to radio, television, and print interviews that soon began to occur with surprising regularity.

All of this was new. We were getting so much business with our media ads all over the airwaves that we had to hire more people. And that meant that we too were starting to put in way more hours than we could find on the clock. I couldn't conceive of any way that any of us could work harder, or smarter, for that matter! But the only thing limiting our income now was the clock. And there was no way we were going to be able to handle all of this business with only two stores. Something had to change, and it had to be quick.

We could see that simply opening more stores for ourselves was going to quickly grow into a management nightmare. Our strengths were excellent products and high-quality service. If we bumped ourselves upstairs to an overseer management position, leaving customer service to personnel who were simply not invested in the success of our business as passionately as we were, we could see that the quality of what we do was going to go down. Maybe it's a pride thing, but I rather believe that it was simply a sound business decision to look someplace else other than opening more stores for ourselves.

So what do you do? You realize the importance of keeping a high integrity business model, but know that you can't handle any more outlets than you already have. We kept thinking.

Franchises

In time, the idea of offering Wesley Berry Flowers franchises started peeking in the window as an alternative. It would help handle the increased business, but the pride of ownership of a financially-invested franchisee would more likely uphold our tradition of great product and high-quality customer service. There was really only one problem. I didn't know a doggone thing about the franchising business.

If you can imagine the world back that far, as I've already mentioned, there was no internet in those days. "Google Search" back then was called the library. So that's where I went once again. I was disappointed, though, to find that there really wasn't much on franchising. I had a little more luck in the bookstore's business section, but still it wasn't all that great. But it was a start. I bought, read, and studied everything they had. It was just a little seed, a rather small beginning, but it did get the franchise ball rolling, and my mind began to feel the sharpening of the grindstone in an area of business that was formerly completely foreign to me.

Then, in the back of a couple of those books, the authors had listed bibliographies, other books that they had referenced. So, naturally, it only made sense to buy and read those books too. To be sure, they were all a big help.

But theory is a lot different than practice. After this small mountain of research, I did certainly understand the concept of franchising a lot better. It was a good step in the right direction. But I still wasn't confident that I could put together a solid, legally sound, nuts and bolts package for our own prospective franchisees. I knew there were quite a few successful franchises already out there, but I was looking for something a lot smaller than the mega-ones like McDonalds and Little Caesar's Pizza.

Like Leo said, when you constantly focus on something, when you keep it continually at the front of your mind as you go about your daily routine, you start to see things in a different light. You start to see things from the perspective of one who's looking for a specific solution to a specific problem. In my case, how does one set up a small business franchise?

I can tell you that I felt an awful lot of frustration. I could see that franchising was a real possibility for our expansion, but I felt too unfamiliar with it. I knew it would be a significant risk if we didn't do it right and the whole thing fell flat for us, or worse, ended up getting us into unforeseen serious legal or financial trouble with some of our future franchisees.

So I took the next step. I began to ask around until it struck me that I could learn a heckuva lot more by soliciting franchise materials—the entire prospective franchisee package—if I simply applied to a variety of existing, already-successful franchisers! So that's what I did.

But I had to be careful to have them NOT send it directly to me, or even in my name. If you're familiar with a Bresser's Directory, easily available to any business, then you know that when someone has your address, they can easily find your name. And a "Wes Berry," uh, of Wesley Berry Flowers, would likely raise enough suspicion to keep most franchisers from mailing out anything to me.

Instead, I asked my pastor's daughter if I could use his address at the parsonage. She was working for me at the time and was happy to agree. The pastor and I were pretty good friends, so I had them send those franchisee packages to one *Herman T.G. Shepherd*. I'll tell you about Herman T.G. Shepherd in an upcoming chapter. Suffice it for now just to tell you that Herman T.G. Shepherd was one of the best dogs I have ever had the pleasure to work with and train. He was…uh…The German (T.G.) Shepherd, and I called him Herman.

I quickly received a cargo-shipload of established franchises' information. In a matter of only a few weeks of doggone diligent study, I probably understood more about how franchises worked than most franchisees. I don't tell you that because I'm some ultra-brilliant student. I tell you that only to say that what I did is something that anybody and his brother could do too. Once again, it was a small beginning. And yet, it was a crucial first step down a whole new path of success for us.

Without going into any further details, unnecessary for this particular discussion, let me conclude this section of my whirlwind story by telling you that we eventually grew to have thirty franchises in five states. And, as you might imagine, our profit margin began to grow exponentially.

But here's the funny thing about it all. Eventually—many years later—we ended up closing up every one of those franchises. Sure, Wesley Berry Flowers did very, very well with them. But, believe it or not, that's not really where the lion's share of our corporate income actually ended up coming from. Something else happened just shortly after that, and so we had to open our minds one more time, and adjust our business model once again. I can imagine that, now, anyone looking back would say that the obvious answer was staring right at us. But back then, …it just wasn't yet.

The Internet

For the purpose of this discussion, I'll just tell you that what happened to our business was about to happen to every other business in a very short time. Around about 1994, a major innovation in the business world was just beginning to attract the notice of alert business leaders all over the world. And those of us who had kept our eyes open, and our ears and minds to the future, were the ones who enjoyed the tremendous advantages this new concept afforded, especially when its value was perceived and utilized by us well before the mainstream crowd was able to grasp its immense importance. It was a monumental new tool that was being made available to all of us for the very first time in history. I'm talking, of course, about the internet. It was a startling new form of technology, an entirely new form of communication that tended to level the playing field for all of us. For the first time in history, a Mom and Pop shop could compete on the same playing field as the big dogs, at least when it came to advertising what they had to offer.

But, as might be expected, not everyone took a shine to this zany new internet thing. Where the heck was it, anyway, this virtual highway to potentially every single household in the world?

For those of us raised and schooled with pen and paper, this was a real head-scratcher.

Regardless, though, I could readily see the opportunity that was staring us in the face. The question was, how to access it. What could we do with all of its potential?

Not all of our competitors took a liking to this new-fangled cyber-world. They'd been successful for many years just doing what they always did, and they couldn't see any overwhelming reason to change just because some people now wanted to do business in this new unseen world.

The internet created an awful lot of chaos for everyone in business back then. But, recall what we were saying back in Chapter 1 on ambition: how chaos has a way of uncovering all kinds of unforeseen new opportunities.

Well, I kept myself well aware of that, and I began my research again. What is this internet thing, and what can we do with it?

Long story short, in 1995 I launched our internet business. We set out with all due diligence, and with laser-focused energy, to develop a formidable, efficient, and necessarily customer-friendly internet presence. After all, it was new to our customers too, wasn't it?

And, to be honest, in retrospect, maybe it wasn't the most sophisticated back then, but it was a wonderful, albeit small beginning for us, on an entirely new business path. In an amazingly short time, it turned out that that's where the customers were starting to hang out more and more. We had to go where our customers were if we hoped to keep the ones we had, and to continue to grow our customer base, as we had been so far, year after year.

And, here's the upshot of that relatively small beginning.

It became quickly apparent that many of our best competitors did not develop their own internet presence. Therefore, most of our new customers, those who had seen the convenience of purchasing their flowers online, examining our inventory without having to leave their kitchen table, and paying without having to get in the car and take the time to stop in and actually see us in person, could not purchase their favorite flowers through their old outlets as easily as they could through Wesley Berry Flowers. In a remarkably short time, we were inundated with new customers. We suddenly found ourselves ahead in a new game, the great new game of e-commerce.

Even more significant for our business, was the fact that the leveling of the playing field allowed us to compete now in a worldwide market, racking up sales from coast to coast and around the globe with millions of customers in over 150 countries. Our internet presence continued to expand from that fledgling beginning, and soon included multiple brands, although Flower Delivery Express emerged as our flagship.

And all of this because of that small beginning. We kept a watchful eye on everything around us, constantly measuring how changes in the world, and especially in the world of business, might affect our business, positively and negatively. We knew well that both possibilities existed. It was up to us to make sure we took advantage of the potential positives. As a consequence, our competitors, those who refused to open their minds to the new possibilities in a rapidly changing world, got stuck with the negative impacts of these same changes.

The end result of all of this? I mentioned earlier in this chapter that in only six months, by beginning with some very small, wholly inexpensive actions (the radio and TV station contacts), our profit grew from a limiting $60 thousand dollars per year to a very rewarding $500 thousand dollars per year.

In 1994, probably to my parents' great joy and relief, I bought out their remaining shares, saw them able to retire in comfort, and I continued down the road.

After the adjustment for our franchise operations, opening, and then eventually closing them out many years later, and then even more after our fledgling commitment to understand and capitalize on the new internet of business, Wesley Berry Flowers eventually grew into Flower Delivery Express. By the time I decided to retire and divest myself of all my business interests, my businesses had totaled more than $750-million-dollars in sales.

I don't mind telling you it was one helluva ride.

Chapter 7— Know Your Working Tools!

You'll recall, perhaps, that back in Chapter 2 we took a look at the unique, wonderfully advantageous business environment we enjoy in America. It's the best of capitalism backed up with a reasonably just democracy. We have rules primarily intended to incentivize business creativity, rules that reasonably protect our business ventures, and rules that are generally intended to have us all play on a level, reasonably fair field of competiton.

Let me just start by reaffirming with a couple of exclamation marks that, without American exceptionalism, free enterprise would simply not exist. Nothing else, no other system of government or of economics has ever created the flood of innovation that America does. We do it a lot, and we do it very well.

Along with that, though—that is, along with innovation— comes a mountain of frequent and often-unexpected change. You just can't have one without the other. Innovation creates something new, and "new" itself is a change. Change is a constant in free enterprise.

Here's a quick, but probably common, example.

For quite a few years in my own business, I used to do what everybody else in business had to do. I diligently kept myself organized by stopping into the office supply store every November or so and picking up my new day-timer for the coming year. And, like most of us, I'd always look for the day-timer that had a bunch of blank pages in the back so I wouldn't be at a loss when I had to write something down. And, it's funny to me now, but I still catch myself trying to make sure I have enough change in the center console. Funny, because I don't think anyone in business has used a pay phone in some twenty years, thank God. Today, of course, every one of those tasks is much more efficiently handled by our smart phones.

And I remember meeting after meeting back then batting around a whirlwind variety of marketing ideas: TV ads, billboards, mailed-out fliers, postal solicitations, and countless others. Like all respectable businesses, we shelled out a lot of money for Yellow Pages ads in those days. You had to! Everybody did. And it worked! The larger the ad, the better it worked.

Today, though, I suppose a business could take out an entire full-page ad in those Yellow Pages, and I imagine almost nobody would see it.

But, with all those marketing strategy meetings back then, not once did the internet come up—social media, websites, Instagram, Pinterest, Facebook. But that's only because they didn't exist yet. Once the internet knocked on our doors, however, we either answered, or else we let the world pass us by. Because, as I've already shown you in the previous chapter, even if we chose not to educate ourselves in the workings and worth of the internet, we could be assured that our competitors would...eventually.

The Electronic Office

Have you had a chance to read through Thomas Friedman's innovative treatment of this very topic in his 2005 work, *The World Is Flat*? This highly-respected, award-winning New York Times columnist put his finger, and his polished intuitive mind, on all the same things that a few of us business leaders were also seeing. He explained, in eye-opening, yet clearly understandable language, how the playing field back then had been leveled on a global scale.

I found myself shaking my head rather vigorously in agreement as I read it, and thinking to myself, "with all we've become aware of in our own business, I too could have written this same book! …yeah, if I wasn't so busy living it!" Unfortunately, I *was* a little busy back then, precisely with that: handling our rapidly-expanding e-commerce business.

However, the book did make it clear that, when the concepts of our newly-flattened world became general knowledge in the world of business, it was likely that our competition would begin to ramp up. I did take some measured solace, however, in the fact that our keen watchfullness and diligence had put us at the head of the great game, at least for that one world-altering innovative moment. I'd certainly rather be leading the pack than trying to catch up to it.

In fact, as should be obvious, most of our competitors did soon follow suit. It wasn't so much a matter of who adapted. It was more a matter of whose adaptations were manifested the quickest, and who was the most innovative and creative in its use.

And so the innovation goes on.

The cycle of change in business used to happen about every five to ten years. Not now. Now it's more like every five to ten months; sometimes even quicker.

So, is such rapid change a good thing or a bad thing for business? How about for society? For families? For life?

For my part, although I certainly have become well aware of both the good and the bad of such rapid change, I've gotta say, I absolutely love it!

I can use social media to play on exactly the same playing field—the entire world—as the largest, most powerful companies in the world. That gives me leverage, not based so heavily on how much money or manpower I can throw at a problem, but based on how much quality I can bring to my work, whether product or service. The little guy today has just as much of a chance to compete as the big guy. I know, because I did!

But what works so well today may not work at all in ninety days. That's key. And that's why anyone in business today has to maintain an aggressive attitude, has to be willing to engage both potential customers and one's own competition.

And you know as well as I that we've all seen this in our personal lives as well. Do you have as many shoe boxes and old photo albums as I do filled with fading photos of your kids' birthday parties, little league games, and those so-cute-you-can't-stand-it dance recitals? What the heck took them so long to invent smart phones with 12-pixel cameras, anyway, right?

And now all my shoe boxes have been moved up to the cloud. Hmph, sure beats the dusty attic.

Whoever could have imagined just a decade or two ago that we'd be showing complete strangers our entire photo album collection just by swiping our fingers left or right across a piece of plastic? Or…ahem…can you imagine twenty years ago telling a friend that you might one day end up marrying someone just because you found yourself swiping a few photos of them on that same piece of plastic? They'd have thought you were nuts! And with good reason, too! I used to think that "dating in the cloud" was a lame reference to the afterlife! Go figure.

And here's another thing that always blows me away. It's that we essentially have all the knowledge of the world, garnered since the very dawn of humankind, right in the palm of our hands! Makes me kind of sad for a guy like me who used to really love his Encyclopedia Brittanica. Well, at least until it went out of date.

Here's another one. I just love maps. Always have. I find them fascinating. All my life, I've had the sense that they had some crazy ability to mentally take me to anywhere on the face of the Earth. It was like I was in a glass airplane flying high overhead, looking down at my hometown, or my state, or my entire country. Loved it!

But now…well…I don't really need them, do I? We've got GPS satellites, and Google Maps, and even a very pleasant tour guide lady inside those handy smart phones who, in fact, never gets bothered when I screw up a turn or two enroute to wherever. She knows details about streets and houses and businesses and restaurants and everything that I could never absorb just by studying a map. And I can do this in my home town, or maybe in Siberia, or Tahiti, or anywhere else on the globe! Why look at a map to get a sense of awe of our world when I can just jump on YouTube and get an actual look from the International Space Station—in real time!

Yeah, things are changing, and they're changing fast. I used to get frustrated driving into the office because I'd really rather have been mentally prepping myself for the presentation, or the meetings that lie ahead that day. Hmph, as I write this, I'm wondering if, by the time you read it, you'll be doing so in a self-driven car as you sip some coffee, scroll through your laptop, and maybe get in a few preparatory phone calls on the way. More power to ya, because it will happen.

Stay on that cutting edge. Success absolutely requires it.

Here's a quick repeat example to emphasize a point: As I've told you already, when the internet began to rear its amazing head in the world of business, we knew we had to do all we could to educate ourselves in its maximum use to reach our customers.

That's where our customers suddenly began popping up, including thousands upon thousands of new ones. We recognized the opportunity, we became thoroughly engaged, and we very soon ended up increasing our customer base many, many times over. And the great majority of those new customers were ones that we had learned to serve in ways that their former suppliers had not yet. We met them WHERE THEY WERE! And they were on the net. So we competed successfully, even with a bunch of the big boys in our field, simply because the playing field had been leveled, and we had learned how to play this new game. And, as I've already said, those of our competitors who had grown complacent with their traditional, long-term strategy, were the very ones from whom our new customers arrived.

Believe it or not, I'm over fifty. And I know well the jokes our society has about people over a certain age being incompetent when it comes to electronic tools. Everybody's going to tell you to be sure to hire at least a couple of under-thirty-somethings, or else there will be nobody to turn to when a computer doesn't work, or maybe the conference room TV screen, or the Powerpoint remote, or a million other things that have to be plugged in or charged up to operate.

If you buy that, I pity you. I really mean it.

If you think that you don't have the ability to study and learn whatever you need to learn to succeed in your business, then I pity you. I mean, to my mind, it doesn't amount to a hill of beans whether or not you can compete with your 14-year-old in a video game! Sure, it'll be fun, and probably pretty cool parenting even, to sit alongside your son in his own world and have some fun together. Sweet. But that's not going to move your business forward! But a whole lot of other capabilities with electronics most certainly will.

A critical element of any business is competition, and it can be mighty fierce. And you can bet your bottom dollar that your competiton is working every bit as hard as you are to grab more market share than you can.

New tools aren't developed for business because they look cool. They're developed because some innovative entrepreneur found out that people had a need, and it was a need that he could concoct a solution for. His cool new gadget was invented first and foremost because it will do a job that you need to do more efficiently, and usually within less time. If it's something that will help you, then get it, and learn to use it.

In my years in the business, I was always amazed and delighted when I came across some program or device or machine or whatever else that would make our business work a little more smoothly, or maybe do something more accurately, more simply, and just a whole lot quicker.

Can you imagine doing business today without computers? I can, but right now I'm really not so sure how, to tell you the truth. I actually had to learn how to type *AFTER* I left school. Talk about a handicap, right? Although today I don't think anyone learns to type anymore. I think we all keyboard now. I used to think electronic typewriters were an absolute wonder! And those little bottles of white-out with them!

To be sure, Word Processing has changed our business world in ways that most of can no longer remember. In fact, so have applications like PowerPoint, Access, Publisher, Photoshop, InDesign, and so many more. I urge you to find out which ones people in your business have incorporated into their work, and then take the time to develop the necessary fluency with each of them.

Now maybe you don't have to actually be the one to do the initial setup on something like Access, but at least know what it can do for you, and how you can avail yourself of what it offers for your own needs for the business.

And, while we're at it, please get as familiar as a teenager with all the capabilities you hold in your hand every day with your smart phone. That little gem is a marvel of scientific genius. You're holding essentially all the wisdom and knowledge in the history of the world in a piece of plastic in your palm. And you can reach, and be reached by just about anyone anywhere in the world by punching in ten or so little numbers on that thing. Use it to its fullest advantage.

But it's not just electronic tools that you need to master.

Leaders

If you want to lead, you must study successful, effective leaders. And don't just watch what they do, watch also how they do it!

For example, one quality every effective leader must master is the ability to speak in front of an audience, even if the audience is only your several employees to start. You must know how to prepare an effective presentation, not just the subject matter itself, but nearly as importantly, the style, tools, and techniques you're going to use to effect real communication with that specific group.

I relish an accomplished speaker, almost regardless of the topic she's speaking on. I watch what gestures she uses, whether or not she uses stories, if she solicits audience participation, if she uses a couple of props for special effect. I take notes on her use of tools sometimes as much as I do on her subject matter. What does she do that really reaches her audience? Is she persuasive? Is she convincing? What techniques does she use to grab the audience's attention? What does she intersperse in her presentation to hold their attention? Does she present herself as sincere, knowledgeable, yet open-minded and approachable? Those are some of the qualities I know I need to develop in myself if I'm going to expect those I'm speaking to to take my words to heart.

Believe it or not, some of the best public speakers in the world were once terribly shy and downright scared to get in front of an audience. If that's you right now, please trust me to know that many before you have confronted that fear head on and have succeeded beyond their wildest dreams in their ability to communicate and move an audience. You can too! It's simply a matter of overcoming the fear to try, then to prepare sufficiently, and then to practice and practice and practice. It takes guts. But then, so does running a business, as you well know. Start small, remember? Maybe your first talk will be in front of a mirror. Okay, so what have we been saying about small beginnings?

And be assured that there are many different avenues for you to use to develop these skills, not least of which is

Toastmasters International, or maybe even the ubiquitous Dale Carnegie courses.

And I can tell you from experience, there are few more wonderful feelings than when you've been able to stand in front of your employees and win them over to some principle or practice that they may have never adopted or accepted were it not for your ability to communicate its necessity or advantages to them and the business. That's leadership at its best.

The Written Word

Did I mention books yet? How about magazines? No matter what field you are in, no matter what your business is, you've got to know that there are a ton of books written about it, and at least a couple dozen magazines or trade journals, usually also available on the web, that keep its practitioners up to date with any new developments in that specialized field. Find out what they are, and be sure to get familiar with them. Then pick out the ones that you feel are essential for keeping your own work on the cutting edge, and make sure they come into your mailbox or email inbox regularly.

Don't forget about business books in general. I guess I don't have to dwell on that one too much, though, seeing as how you are reading this one. Nice work.

Time spent honing your skills, gaining sufficient competency with all of the tools available to you, electronic and otherwise, is time that will pay off for you in spades, in ways that will likely surprise you when they all of a sudden turn up to solve a problem for you.

Sure it takes time to master these things. But remember the little story about the brutish new axman in the northwoods timber-cutting crew. He felt since he was bigger and stronger than every other man on that crew, he should be honored as such and paid the most because of it. But his foreman pointed out that that small guy sitting on the bench over there was actually the one who chopped the most wood for this crew, so he was the one to beat.

Of course, our hero set out to do just that, coming in earlier and staying later out in the woods chopping continuously until he was sure he had out-chopped the little champion, a guy who he noticed used to sit down to rest a whole lot more than he needed to. Looked like a piece of cake.

But day after day the little champ always chopped more wood.

So when the new brute, in his agonized frustration, asked the foreman how that could possibly be, he was finally told that the little champ didn't really sit down to rest. What he was doing while he sat was sharpening his axe.

That's something we all have to do too, with whatever tools we have at our disposal. For leaders, there aren't too many tools that can't be learned when we put our minds to it. And if we're going to play the great game, we're likely going to need every one of them.

Chapter 8—Listen! ...and Learn:
Understanding Others

Last summer, I stopped into a Dairy Queen. It's funny, but I always feel like I'm cheating on my wife when I do that. When you're cheating like that, it seems the lines never move fast enough. I mean, she might happen to drive by, right? Besides, as I recall, that particular day was one of those Michigan ninety-degree days, and ice cream always seems to soften the blow.

As I waited in line, up ahead of me were two adults, and one of them was really starting to annoy people all around her, including me, quite frankly. She was turning around and asking anyone she came in contact with all sorts of lame questions.

"Is this your first time here?"

"What kind of ice cream do *YOU* like?"

"Are you gonna get just plain ice cream or are you gonna get it with different toppings on it?"

As you know, in most circles, it's pretty common protocol to just wait for your ice cream, and mind your own business while you wait. Everybody knows that. Some people, I guess, just never read the memo, y'know?

Then, just to tick the rest of us off a little more, I think, she finally gets her ice cream, and immediately starts complaining that she ordered one with sprinkles, and there are no sprinkles on hers, and that's not what she ordered, and what happened there, anyway!

At long last, the second person finally turns around. And she walks her adult daughter, probably about thirty-five years old and obviously mentally challenged, over to a table to enjoy their ice cream together. The daughter was just soooo happy to be at that dairy queen. Until that moment, though, I had no idea whatsoever that she was mentally handicapped. Of course, I immediately mentally slapped myself up the side of the head.

It's really easy, isn't it, to judge somebody when we don't have all the facts? And it's a lot easier still when we don't have any obligation to actually engage with them. I wasn't in business with this woman, didn't have to work with her, didn't have to have any interaction with her at all! But, when I realized why she was acting as she was, when I did acquire a few more of the facts, I felt like a louse for even thinking that I wished she'd quit bothering everybody.

This young woman was soooo close to passing as NOT having a handicap that we all should have applauded that alone. I can only begin to imagine all the time, work, energy, and effort both she and her mother had put in for those last 35 years or so to help her to that point. But it struck me then that, if this woman had instead been paralyzed and maybe unable even to speak a word, I wouldn't have thought anything of being patient with her.

It's really unfair, isn't it, to judge others without fully understanding what they're grappling with?

Allow me to borrow another example from the writings of business guru Stephen Covey from his *7 Habits of Highly Effective People.*

He tells of the time he was sitting quietly on a train heading into the city, when a couple of unusually disruptive kids appeared in his car, and started running around, talking real loud, climbing over the seats, and stuff like that. Obviously, it started to really irritate him. He says he began to scowl at their father, a man who seemed far too passive to exert any authority, or even minimal control, over his own children! Covey had a mind to give that guy a piece of his own mind!

Then, he says, the father came up to Covey and apologized to him for his children's behavior.

"I'm sorry," he began. "But my kids just lost their mother this morning, and I'm afraid we're all at a loss for the moment about how we're going to go on without her."

I imagine Covey felt about the same way I did with my ice cream friend.

But here's the point. It is essential, and yet often extremely difficult sometimes, to see things from the perspective of others. We all have our own paradigms, our own view of our business, our family, our world.

It's All About Perspective

You might say we all wear our own unique glasses, and those glasses have filters on them that arise out of our own unique experiences of the world. But everyone wears their own one-of-a-kind pair of glasses. Nobody sees anything in exactly the same way as we do. Therefore, if we're to understand how to work with others, how to train others, how to communicate with others, to problem-solve with others, and even to compete with others, it's going to be incredibly important to be able, as much as possible, to see things through their particular glasses. It's true that an inner mindset can be crucial for exploring all the fine nuances of a problem. But it is often equally important to go outside of that necessarily-limited mindset to broaden your view to include that of others.

And why is this so necessary? Because every one of us, especially leaders, need to look out for those situations where our own paradigm is giving us inappropriate feedback. In other words, it will always be helpful in decision-making to measure your own perspective on a problem against the different perspectives of those who are also involved in that problem.

Simple case in point: many of us teach our kids that when they get lost or come across some other trouble, to just look for a policeman or policewoman to help them out. It's always a safe bet, we tell them. BUT, that certainly may NOT be true for someone who has seen excessive abuse by police, sometimes a minority person, or, as in some cases I've come across, someone who has immigrated to the U.S. from a military dictatorship. To them, police may be seen more as the enemy, or at least as someone to stay as far away from as possible.

Let's face facts here. We all have some handicap, limitation, or idiosyncrasy that we casually, probably subliminally ask others to put up with. It might not be readily visible, and may well be the result of some previous successes or failures of our own. All of that ends up forming us into who we are on any given day. As it turns out, we too are constantly asking others to understand our worldview as well as we need to understand theirs, especially if we need to work together toward a common goal.

I used to do a little exercise with my employees that I picked up from James C. Collins' business mega-hit book *Good to Great: Why Some Companies Make the Leap ...and Others Don't*

(William Collins, 2001). He used a fun little drawing done by William Ely Hill back in 1915 that Hill titled, *My Wife and My Mother-in-Law,* to illustrate the principle of an object showing considerably different perspectives on exactly the same thing. If you've read the book, maybe you remember this drawing?

Depending on your point of view, especially your very first impression, is it a young woman looking to her left, or an elderly woman looking down? Could be either, right?

Anyway, I'd show this to half the audience with introductory words something like, "Just to illustrate a point, take a look at this drawing of an elderly woman." Then I'd show the same drawing to the other half of the audience with the words, "Now look at this drawing of a pretty young woman."

Of course, I'd show both sides of the audience, unknown to one another though, the exact same picture. When I'd then follow this with showing everyone together that same drawing for the second time, it was always startling, to me and to the audience themselves, how many simply could not alter their original point of view. If they first saw the elderly woman, many just could not see the young woman, and vice versa. Most could…but not all.

There's no question that we are heavily conditioned by our own unique background, upbringing, and life experiences. The power of successful leadership, however, comes in large part with your development of the ability to see something from the other's point of view. Only then can real communication, and real problem-solving, begin.

When I was in high school, I joined the debate team. Forensics. I liked it, so I worked pretty hard at it, and I got pretty good. I liked to take the position of first affirmative, the one who begins the debate by laying out the arguments *for* a position. But then I also got a kick out of taking the "second negative" position, causing me to bring out all the arguments *against* that same position. I'll tell you, that is one heckuva way to learn to see things from a wholly different perspective.

In fact, I used to occasionally help my kids understand the same concept at our dinner table. My wife is Chinese, so my kids are half German, half Chinese. One day I asked them to debate the merits of eating their meal with forks over eating with chopsticks, two methods with which they were all comfortably familiar. I was amazed at how much fun we all had with something as crazy as that. But I also know that it helped to cement a very important concept in my kid's heads. It helped them to see both sides.

As you may already know, this is a basic concept when it comes to sales. You've got to be able to understand where your potential customer is coming from, what THEIR needs are, not what your needs are in your hopes to make a sale. And at the same time, you've got to know both the pluses and minuses of your own product or service if you're going to be sufficiently prepared to handle the questions and objections you know are likely to arise. First affirmative and second negative, right?

So, how do you go about it? Well, listening well comes to mind as a very important first step. But you might also try putting yourself intentionally into situations or conversations that you wouldn't normally enter into. If you're a Republican, seek out the opinion on any issue of a Democrat, or maybe of a Libertarian. If you're a Christian, maybe do a little study to help you understand the basics of the Jewish faith, or maybe Islam, or Hindu, or any other that seems confusing to you.

And if you're dead-set sure that project A has always been done this way and that there's no good reason to do it any other way, may I suggest you seek out somebody who is willing to look at another way of doing it, and LISTEN. Listen with your mind wide open.

I'm not saying you have to agree! But I am saying you owe it to yourself as a leader to listen without internally knocking down every little step they take to explain their proposal. Listen—with an OPEN mind—to everything they're saying. Then spend a little time thinking about it. If you end up not completely agreeing with their suggestion, is there perhaps a way that you can combine what they've come up with together with what has always been done to improve the overall process? Remember that no progress can be made without change, and no change is ever made without some discomfort and some risk.

It's understandably a pretty tall order for anyone, but whether it's in your family life, personal life, or in your business, I'd recommend strongly that, if you're serious about learning to play in the great game, you seek first to understand, before you try to be understood. Successful leaders do not exist without that capability. You will never understand your own position as well as when you also learn to understand and appreciate a different point of view.

The Prisoner, by
Francisco de Goya
Lucientes, 1867.
Goya was an original
and enigmatic artist,
equally gifted as a
painter and a
printmaker. This
etching has always
held a special
fascination for me,
principally because
of the hidden image
it contains. Take a
close look. Maybe you can see what demon really torments our
prisoner. If it escapes you, check out page 258.

Chapter 9—Controlling the Battlefield!

I was at a business conference once during which the speaker invited a volunteer up to the front to help him out with a brief demonstration.

He presented the volunteer with a sealed envelope into which he told us he had put a single playing card. Then, without allowing her to open the envelope yet, he began to ask her a couple of questions.

"Would you pick any two suits of playing cards, please?"

She chose spades and hearts.

"Good choice. Would you now think about both of those two suits, and please choose just one of them?"

She chose spades.

"Okay, now would you please pick any four cards, face or number, and tell me what they are?

She chose ace, king, 9, and 2.

"Good," he said. "Would you now select any two of those four cards, please?"

She chose the king and the 2.

"Wonderful," he told her. "Now I'd like you to eliminate the two you've selected, and choose only one of the other two."

She eliminated, of course, the king and the 2, leaving her with the ace and the 9. Of those, she then chose the 9.

"Excellent," he said. "Now that's the one I'd like you to eliminate, and then please open the envelope."

Of course, she was left with naming the Ace of Spades, and, lo and behold, that was the card in the envelope.

It's not very difficult to see what was happening here, is it?

The presenter was very methodically controlling the conversation. In leading her to choose the Ace of Spades—the end goal of the exercise—he simply asked her either to keep a selection she'd made if it led in that direction, or else to eliminate the selection she'd made if it led away from the end target.

Simple enough, but he was visually demonstrating for us a pretty powerful point, the importance of controlling the game, controlling the playing field so that you always keep a little bit of an edge.

I've already mentioned to you that I attended a few years of military school, so forgive me if my illustrations come from that discipline. I do find, however, that they are shining examples of what this chapter is all about. And it's about how so often the slightest advantage can make all the difference. That's why fighter pilots are taught to attack with the sun behind their backs whenever possible. Let that infernal blinding sun be in their adversaries' eyes!

And history is replete with situations that beautifully illustrate this very principle.

Take a look at this one, for instance.

Sam Houston

During the War for Texas Independence in 1836, Sam Houston (1793-1863), began to organize his meager, ramshackle Texas army for combat. He was the newly appointed Commander-in-Chief of the Army of Texas, still a territory in dispute with Mexico at the time. The fledgling Texas volunteer militia was coming fresh out of the notorious defeat at the Alamo on March 6 of that year, and now Houston and his men were going to have to defend the Texas territory from the superior numbers and disciplined experience of the Mexican troops under seasoned General Lopez Antonio de Santa Anna (1794-1876), who was also Mexico's president at that time.

Houston was given only 374 poorly trained, poorly outfitted, and poorly supplied men to command in his imminent confrontation with the advancing Santa Ana army of more than 1,500, fresh and confident from their overwhelming defeat of the Texas militia at the Alamo.

To make this rather long story short, Houston looked at what he had to work with and developed his strategy. Heavily outnumbered and outclassed, to say the least, he continually retreated away from the relentlessly approaching army of Santa Anna. The rains came nearly every day in Texas as his army retreated, and the combination of miserable conditions, poor supplies and rations, and the debilitating, cowardly-appearing retreating of his men began to take its serious toll on their morale.

But Sam Houston had a plan. He needed to buy time to build his army, and he knew that the devastation and cruelty shown by Santa Anna in one Texas town after another would end up being quite an incentive for more and more belligerent Texans to join his campaign, which they did.

Eventually, he found the field of battle he had been looking for, and finally his recruits grew to about 800 strong, against Santa Ana's now 900 or so, but soon reinforced to a total of about 1,300. But Houston knew that Santa Anna was eager to pursue and engage him and finally end this war and return to his presidency in

Mexico. He knew Santa Anna would follow him wherever he might lead him.

So he led his army into a large, only partially forested area surrounded on all sides by waterways: either rivers, lakes, or marshes. They no longer would be able to escape any further. However, they did have the significant advantage of being able to set up their camp among heavy oaks, which not only shielded them from easy attack, but also concealed their limited numbers from the enemy.

On the contrary, Santa Anna was forced to enter that same limited space, set up his own army's camp no more than about 500 yards from Houston's, with only a small hill concealing one army from the other, and in an area completely unprotected by any forest cover at all.

Further, Houston had learned that Santa Anna had split his army into three parts so as to surround the Texans and finish them off. So, he knew the time to act was now, against this limited fragment of the entire Mexican army, and with their supreme commander present. He also knew that Mexican reinforcements were on the way.

The Mexican reinforcements soon did arrive, at 9:00am on the morning of April 21st, bringing Santa Anna's total troop count back up to between 1,300-1,500 strong. However, Houston knew that those reinforcements had been marching continually for the last twenty-four hours straight through the heavily mud-laden roads, some of which were so bad as to force the soldiers to trek through them knee-deep in mud. Therefore, after confirming their arrival, he had his men destroy the bridge that led into the battle area, about eight miles behind Santa Anna's army encampment.

Now there was no escape for the Mexican army either, and Houston had the better ground and cover as an advantage. Besides, his men had been waiting there for nearly two weeks now, fully healed up and rested.

He spent the day in preparation, intentionally leading Santa Anna to believe that there would be no attack that day, but very likely it would wait until dawn. After keeping his exhausted men continually at alert for that entire morning, and the first half of the afternoon, Santa Anna finally relented and allowed them to take a break, get some sleep, and clean themselves up a little.

And that's when Houston signaled to begin his attack. His first cannon shot took place at 4:30 that afternoon. The startled, overwhelmed Mexican army began an immediate retreat, and they were immediately pounced on and pursued into the marshes by the Texans, who kept up their merciless barrage against "anything that moved" until no less that 650 Mexicans were killed, and 300 were captured. In Houston's army, only eleven men died and thirty were injured, including, however, Houston himself who was wounded in his ankle. The whole battle was over in just eighteen minutes. And, because of it, Texas won its independence.

Why do I use this as an example?

Because it illustrates the power of picking the battlefield, the power of preparation, and the power of knowing your competition, and playing to your own strengths, whatever they might be, as you attempt to minimize the strengths of your competition…er, uh, enemy, in this case.

Almost every military engagement involves a decision as to where and when any battle is going to take place. It's not just on the battlefield itself, though.

We talked about Rome in an earlier chapter on ambition. They were certainly formidable in their day. But some of the biggest thorns in their side were Hannibal and his pesky Carthaginians across the sea. So, after defeating them, and then seeing them rise up again and start a second war, the Romans decided they needed to find a better way to keep them down than to just return every couple of years and fight a new and costly war with them.

So, after their second defeat of Carthage, the Romans decided to salt their growing fields. That absolutely ruined the ground for any sustenance planting, and very soon afterward the Carthaginians dispersed to various other lands where they could at least survive. They never again were able to form a people formidable enough together to offer any more challenges to the might of Rome.

Now I'm not suggesting that you do that to the gardens of your competitors. There are laws against it; not just civil, but ethical. But it does suggest to us the impact of finding creative solutions to complicated problems, doesn't it?

Okay, so that's war. Luckily, business competition doesn't have to go that far. Healthy competition doesn't need to involve any killing. But I'm talking about the importance of establishing a playing field that can provide you with some significant advantages. Let me offer you an example from my own experience.

Controlling the Battlefield

When I began offering franchises, I had to interview a fair number of possible interested franchisee candidates. I'm sure they hoped to make a good impression on me; but I also knew it was important to have them get a strong impression of our company. I had to control the battlefield.

So, when I would advertise for franchisees in a city outside of Detroit, as we did quite a bit, I would rent a hotel conference room in that city for the interviews. Of course, I'd always get there plenty early to set the room up the way I needed it to be. It's significant which way the chairs face, and even who sits in which chair sometimes. In this case, I was careful to position my own chair so that I could see when the next candidate arrived, usually while I was still interviewing an earlier candidate.

And I'd schedule the various interviews to overlap one another. This way, when my next interviewee would show up while the present interviewee was still present, it cemented the impression, true enough, that we had our fair share of applicants, and that we could be choosy in looking for those who would play the great game with us at an equally high level.

In addition, often when I'd meet with someone from whom I needed something to complement our business, I'd ask an associate, hopefully from a business similar to the one my interviewee represented, to just stop by during the time of the interview, interrupt us and say hi. Then, of course, I'd have to politely introduce him to the prospective associate I was already speaking with, and, sure as shootin', that prospect would hear a bit of an earful about what a great company we were. And he'd hear it from someone usually who was in a business similar to his own. It was a great way to confirm for the prospect that his risk in partnering with us was rather minimal.

Another critical function of leadership in business is to find and help develop more and more leaders for your business at every one of its levels. Even here, it's very helpful to control the battlefield. Let me offer another example; but I'll have to ask you to stick with me on this one until the whole thing is played out here.

Herman, the German Shepard

When I was trying to research franchising, as you might recall, I mentioned that I had franchisers send their information packets to one Mr. Herman T.G. Shepherd. He was my remarkable German Shepherd companion. I named him Herman. But he wasn't yet remarkable when I first got him as a pup. Let me tell you, though, how I went about making him the best dog I've ever owned, and how the principles I employed can also be used to enhance your business relationships.

If you really want to thoroughly train your dog, you've got to allocate the necessary time. You may have the *goal* to train him, but you also have to set specific objectives to accomplish that. Herman was by far the best dog I've ever had, but I know that that's because he's the one I dedicated the most time and energy to in order to train him. I also took the time to attend some dog training classes with Herman, classes conducted by someone who trained dogs for the military.

I was about twenty-one when I started the training, and back then Herman would always sit near me as I worked. I first developed the practice of occasionally calling him, for no particular reason, and when he'd come to me I'd feed him a piece of bologna. I also trained him to take no food from anyone except me, and from his own food bowl. After I'd been doing this thing with the bologna for a week or two, Herman seemed to have made the decision to try to figure out what I wanted from him, what I wanted him to do. In a rather short time, he developed a curiosity about what he had to do to get the bologna. Occasionally, he'd go get a can of dog food for himself and bring it to me.

In our store, pretty much every day there was a brief lull in business at around 10:30am, right after we'd gotten all of our orders out. So I chose that time each day to train Herman on a leash.

I may have mentioned earlier that our Detroit store was in a rather rough neighborhood. Whenever a customer would come into the store, Herman would step out from behind the counter and just sit there watching that customer, observing whatever was going on. At any rate, in a relatively short time, he would do everything I'd command him to…while on his leash.

Off-leash, however, was another matter.

Behind our shop was a small backyard, and there were often puddles all over it. Herman loved water. He thought it was funny to run, and to try to get me to run after him. He was quicker and faster than me, of course, so this would have turned the tables on who's the master here. But he kept at it.

So I thought about it some, and knew I had to get past this little rebellion phase, this tampering with who between us was going to be in charge.

So one day I took him down to the basement and walked him around on the leash for a bit, and then I let him off-leash. Immediately he again began clowning around like he did when we went outside.

As usual, he ran around a little, trying to entice me to come after him. Eventually, he even started back up the stairs, ostensibly to really take off and leave me behind. But I had closed the door at the top of the stairs. When he ran up against it, he suddenly realized he was trapped. And now I was coming up the stairs after him. There was nowhere for him to go.

He became visibly nervous. I'd never struck Herman—never would—but I always made it real clear to him when I was displeased with something he'd done. He knew those signals very well, and always reacted to them in, well, what I'd have to label a peculiar apologetic manner. After all, like all dogs, he really wanted to please his master, and, when he knew he displeased me, it always had an appreciable effect on him.

As I came slowly up the stairs, he knew he had displeased me again. He was visibly trembling, hunkered down a little as if terribly ashamed of his behavior. He actually lost his bladder, making a bit of a mess on those stairs, so sure was he that I was about as disappointed with him as I'd ever been.

Of course, I would never hurt him.

I quietly approached him, calmly put him back on the leash, didn't make any fuss at all about the mess he knew he'd made on the stairs, and then walked him back down the stairs and around

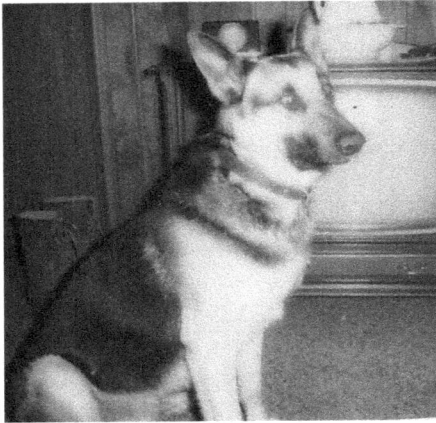

the room a few more times. He stuck right next to me every step of the way. And, yeah, that's him in the photo.

From that day on, Herman made a significant mental change. He had apparently decided that, from now on, he was not going to clown around any more, but was going to comply as well as he could with whatever I might ask of him. And from that day on, he did. In fact, I could have him 100 yards away from me, but could still command him using hand signals, directing him to move left or move right or whatever else was required. From that moment on, Herman was simply the most phenomenal dog I've ever had.

With obvious differences, there are elements of working with a dog that might be instructive when it comes to working with people. Forgive me, but sometimes I wonder how many principles of psychology might apply to both of our species. I know. I know! I'm _not_ comparing people to dogs! Please don't get me wrong. I"m just sayin', …when you get a …champ like Herman, it can't help but get you thinkin'.

Building Trust

Just like with Herman, when you work with people, you certainly first have to build a genuine trust with them. If you can give them what they need to get their job done, they're much more likely to trust you as a leader, and to actually get the job done…the way it needs to be done.

As an example, often when I'd hire a key person for our company, I'd conclude our final hiring interview with a significant cash bonus to them for signing on with us. It was my way of letting them know in no uncertain terms that they were important to me and that I was sincere in my desire to develop a trusting relationship with them.

And that trust will go a long way toward building a company of responsible employees and business partners that you can count on, whether you're present with them or not at any given moment.

At the same time, as we all know, there will certainly be occasions when even a good employee will veer off the path. That's something you may have to control. If that does happen, and you are made aware of it, it's important that, first, they know you're aware of it, but secondly that they also know you don't hold a grudge against them for their having stepped a little off the expected path. You'll have much better results if you can forgive the behavior, and let them know that you do, and that your trust in them hasn't faltered just because of a single mishap. This kind of reaction will go a long way toward building that relationship you're hoping for with a good employee, one whereby you can expand the business by having great employees who are continually assured, and reassured when necessary, of your trust in them.

Let's remember, however, that you yourself can really only do this with people who are directly under you, who answer directly to you. Therefore, it's important, if you're going to build a cohesive company-wide team that can work well together with confidence in one another, that your supervisors do much the same with each of those who answer to them.

Rewards

I hope you can see that thanking or expressing special appreciation for something an employee or associate has done is kind of like feeding the bologna to Herman. Personally, of course, I think it's quite a cut above. Myself, I'm not all that crazy about bologna, anyway. Had a little too much of the stuff when I was a kid back in some of those lean times for our business. But I think you can see what I mean. If an action of an employee or associate is praiseworthy, well, my gosh, praise it, and preferably in public! Let them know you're thankful. Let them know they have greatly honored the trust you have placed in them.

After the praise, it also may be necessary to occasionally pull that same person aside and identify for them what they may have done better. The end game, though, is to reinforce enough confidence in them, coupled with the insight you're offering, to where they themselves can now make the decision to identify *for themselves* what they can do better, without any input from you at all.

If you want to build a successful company, you've got to build successful leaders at every level of that company.

PART III

Seeking Out That Needle in the Haystack

"We choose to go to the moon in this decade and do the other things, not because they are easy, but because they are hard, because that goal will serve to organize and measure the best of our energies and skills..."

John F. Kennedy

Chapter 10—Finding the Right People:
Needle in the Haystack

Next to having a great product or superior service, probably nothing is as important to the success of any business as the people who are hired to make it happen, every one of them. We're talking here about employees, but also about anyone with whom you choose to partner, whether it be attorneys, accountants, or any other non-employee contractors. And any business person knows that the greatest challenge in running a company is to find the right people.

You'd think that would be easy, right? If you've got a business that's already successful, one that allows you to pay a doggone good wage, then you'd think hiring or contracting with good people would be the very least of your problems.

If you've tried it, you know that's simply not true.

I ran a highly successful business for many years. But you know what? Every single day, I would hear all kinds of excuses from one employee or another for not taking responsibility for projects they had been assigned. Success only comes from taking responsibility for your actions, good or bad! I was always amazed at how so many of my employees seemed more interested in avoiding success than making the effort to figure out how to get the job done right. Probably much like you, I didn't really mind so much when somebody took on a special responsibility, tried their best, but maybe failed. It was the avoidance of the responsibility itself that always drove me nuts.

And now, after a lifetime of continually seeking out and nurturing the special, personally responsible employees while weeding out their opposites, I've come to a conclusion. This type of behavior, this avoidance of personal responsibility at all kinds of levels, is a major cause for the underperformance, and often the failure, of way too many companies across this nation.

Simply put, if you want your company to be a leader in your industry or field of commerce, then you need to be able to identify employees who can help you succeed to that level by taking personal responsibility for their assignments. It's critical for you to make this a priority and get involved in this process at the individual employee level. In my humble, but experienced opinion, your future depends on it.

My hope in these next few chapters is to shed a bright light on how you as a manager, business owner, or even department manager, can identify those employees that have the unique ability to take responsibility for tasks that are necessary to be successful in today's complex and fast-paced business world. It is my hope that, after you have read these chapters, you will not only have a better understanding of these unique and special character traits, but you will also learn how to identify those employees in your organization who will assist you with becoming the successful company you are striving to be.

But let me get something straight from the get-go. I am not a professional writer or management consultant. I do not have any degrees in business or management from Harvard or Yale or Stanford or anywhere else. Amazing, right? That anyone could actually be successful without one of their sheepskins is probably close to the ninth Wonder of the World.

To quote Liam Neeson's character from the movie *Taken*, "But what I have are a very particular set of skills, skills I have acquired over a very long career."

My family owned a very successful business for over seventy years, and I have learned during that time that a significant contributor to any business's success is the owner's ability to identify certain character traits in the people you hire. It's a skill that every manager needs to develop.

My intent in writing this is to enable any manager to make a critical judgment regarding the potential of an employee to handle a given assignment, and carry that assignment through to success.

But I like to keep it plain and simple. This isn't a moon shot we're talking about here. There are no long questionnaires to be answered or the need for an expert to interpret the results. As we'll see, only two simple assignments will give you an insight into the ability of any employee.

I will also discuss how to identify, supervise, reward, and train those individuals through simple exercises.

When I found an employee I was considering hiring, I always presented him or her with a short, 1,500-word story, actually written in 1899, entitled *A Message to Garcia* by Elbert Hubbard. It's based on an event that occurred during the Spanish American War. In fact, that story is my next chapter. It's the foundation of this section. If you will be reading it for the first time, or if you perhaps have read it before, you will discover why I have included it, and the value this story has for identifying people who will assist you in developing a successful business.

The story is about Andrew Summers Rowan, an American Army officer who carried out one singularly critical task in that war. But Hubbard's choice to write about this man is based on the character traits that it took for that officer to carry out his mission, character traits that were essential to his success. They're the very same traits that I'm suggesting are important for you and your managers to understand and identify in every one of your employees.

Psychologists and others who study human motivation have a variety of names for the characteristics that Rowan exhibited in the undertaking of his assignment. They may be labeled as "high-need achievers' or as "task-oriented" people by these professionals. Okay, that's probably much more accurate than my own label, but I'm kinda big on keeping things simple whenever possible. I refer to the traits that make a person successful as "Rowan traits." And, let me be clear here: I'm no psychologist. My book is not about explaining the underlying need or reason for Rowans' behavior. My primary intent is to demonstrate how, through a few simple exercises, you will be able to identify people who will be highly productive in your business. You'll fairly easily and accurately be able to seek out the "Rowans" in your own company. And that alone will go a long way toward keeping you on that road to success.

It's key for any company to develop high-quality leaders at

all levels. I had over 100 employees on staff in the United States, and close to 200 employees overseas. I understand rather well the need of managers to have competent and responsible employees that they can rely on to undertake critical assignments. The goal is to aid you in finding them and nurturing them.

Chapter 11—A Message To Garcia

In this chapter, I'd like to tell you a story. No, not mine this time. But one that was written back in 1899 by one Elbert Hubbard. If you get a minute, Google him. He was a fascinating character, not least of all in business.

I think you'll find it instructive. It has been incredibly useful to me over the years as I set about assessing my employees, and I'm sure it'll do the same for you.

But it wasn't just helpful to me. Over 40,000,000 copies of *A Message to Garcia* were printed, suspected of being the largest circulation of any literary venture in history during the lifetime of the author, thanks to a series of lucky accidents.

I could go on and tell you how it came about, and even how it spread. But I really think it makes a lot more sense to allow you to hear about it from the author himself, even before you read the actual story. Here's what Elbert Hubbard said himself about this phenomenal story.

The Writing of "A Message to Garcia," by Elbert Hubbard

This literary trifle, "A Message to Garcia," was

written one evening after supper, in a single hour. It was on the Twenty-second of February, Eighteen Hundred Ninety-nine, Washington's Birthday, and we were just going to press with the March "Philistine." *(ed. note: The Philistine was the monthly publication of which Hubbard was the editor and publisher)* The thing leaped hot from my heart, written after a trying day, when I had been endeavoring to train some rather delinquent villagers to abjure the comatose state and get radio-active.

The immediate suggestion, though, came from a little argument over the teacups, when my boy Bert suggested that Rowan was the real hero of the Cuban War. Rowan had gone alone and done the thing—carried the message to Garcia.

It came to me like a flash! Yes, the boy is right, the hero is the man who does his work--who carries the message to Garcia. I got up from the table, and wrote "A Message to Garcia." I thought so little of it that we ran it in the Magazine without a heading. The edition went out, and soon orders began to come for extra copies of the March "Philistine," a dozen, fifty, a hundred; and when the American news company ordered a thousand, I asked one of my helpers which article it was that had stirred up the cosmic dust.

"It's the stuff about Garcia," he said.

The next day a telegram came from George H. Daniels, of the New York Central Railroad, thus: "Give price on one hundred thousand Rowan article in pamphlet form—Empire State Express advertisement on back—also how soon can ship."

The result was that I gave Mr. Daniels permission to reprint the article in his own way. He issued it in booklet form in editions of half a million. Two or three of these half-million lots were sent out by Mr. Daniels, and in addition the article was reprinted in over two hundred magazines and newspapers. It has been translated into all written languages.

At the time Mr. Daniels was distributing the "Message to Garcia," Prince Hilakoff, Director of Russian Railways, was in this country. He was the guest of the New York Central, and made a tour of the country under the personal direction of Mr. Daniels. The Prince saw the little book and was interested in it, more because Mr. Daniels was putting it out in such big numbers, probably, than otherwise.

In any event, when he got home he had the matter translated into Russian, and a copy of the booklet given to every railroad employee in Russia. Other countries then took it up, and from Russia it passed into Germany, France, Spain, Turkey, Hindustan and China. During the war between Russia and Japan, every Russian soldier who went to the front was given a copy of the "Message to Garcia."

The Japanese, finding the booklets in possession of the Russian prisoner, concluded that it must be a good thing, and accordingly translated it into Japanese.

And of an order of the Mikado, a copy was given to every man in the employ of the Japanese Government, soldier or civilian. Over forty million copies of " A Message to Garcia" have been printed.

E.H.

Pretty cool story, huh? It's almost as good as the story

itself, so let's get to it. Thanks you for your patience. Here's the story Elbert Hubbard wrote that day at the dinner table in under an hour.

MESSAGE TO GARCIA
By Elbert Hubbard

In all this Cuban business there is one man stands out on the horizon of my memory like Mars at perihelion.

When war broke out between Spain and the United States, it was very necessary to communicate quickly with the leader of the Insurgents. Garcia was somewhere in the mountain fastnesses of Cuba—no one knew where. No mail or telegraph message could reach him. The President must secure his co-operation, and quickly. What to do!

Someone said to the President, "There is a fellow by the name of Rowan who will find Garcia for you, if anybody can."

Rowan was sent for and was given a letter to be delivered to Garcia. How "the fellow by the name of Rowan" took the letter, sealed it up in an oilskin pouch, strapped it over his heart, in four days landed by night off the coast of Cuba from an open boat, disappeared into the jungle, and in three weeks came out on the other side of the Island, having traversed a hostile country on foot, and delivered his letter to Garcia—are things I have no special desire now to tell in detail. The point that I wish to make is this: McKinley gave Rowan a letter to be delivered to Garcia; Rowan took the letter and did not ask, "Where is he at?" By the Eternal! There is a man whose form should be cast in deathless bronze and the statue placed in every college of the land. It is not book-learning young men need, nor instruction about this and that, but a stiffening of the vertebrae which will cause them to be loyal to a trust, to act promptly, concentrate their energies: do the thing—"Carry a message to Garcia."

General Garcia is dead now, but there are other Garcias.

No man who has endeavored to carry out an enterprise where many hands were needed, but has been well-nigh appalled at times by the imbecility of the average man—the inability or unwillingness to concentrate on a thing and do it.

Slipshod assistance, foolish inattention, dowdy indifference, and half-hearted work seem the rule; and no man succeeds, unless by hook or crook or threat he forces or bribes other men to assist him; or mayhap, God in His goodness performs a miracle, and sends him an Angel of Light for an assistant. You, reader, put this matter to a test: You are sitting now in your office—six clerks are within call. Summon anyone and make this request: "Please look in the encyclopedia and make a brief memorandum for me concerning the life of Correggio."

Will the Clerk quietly say, "Yes, sir," and go do the task?

On your life he will not. He will look at you out of a fishy eye and ask one or more of the following questions:

Who was he?
Which encyclopedia?
Where is the encyclopedia?

Was I hired for that?

Don't you mean Bismarck?

What's the matter with Charlie doing it?

Is he dead?

Is there any hurry?

Shall I bring you the book and let you look it up yourself?

What do you want to know for?

And I will lay you ten to one that after you have answered the questions, and explained how to find the information, and why you want it, the clerk will go off and get one of the other clerks to help him try to find Garcia—and then come back and tell you there is no such man. Of course I may lose my bet, but according to the Law of Average I will not.

Now, if you are wise, you will not bother to explain to your "assistant" that Correggio is indexed under the C's, not in the K's, but you will smile very sweetly and say, "Never mind," and go look it up yourself.

And this incapacity for independent action, this moral stupidity, this infirmity of the will, this unwillingness to cheerfully catch hold and lift—these are the things that put pure Socialism so far into the future. If men will not act for themselves, what will they do when the benefit of their effort is for all? A first mate with knotted club seems necessary; and the dread of getting "the bounce" Saturday night holds many a worker to his place.

Advertise for a stenographer, and nine out of ten who apply can neither spell nor punctuate—and do not think it necessary to.

Can such a one write a letter to Garcia?

"You see that bookkeeper," said a foreman to me in a large factory.

"Yes; what about him?"

"Well, he's a fine accountant, but if I'd send him up-town on an errand, he might accomplish the errand all right, and on the other hand, might stop at four saloons on the way, and when he got to Main Street would forget what he had been sent for."

Can such a man be entrusted to carry a message to Garcia?

We have recently been hearing much maudlin sympathy expressed for the "down-trodden denizens of the sweat-shop" and the "homeless wanderer searching for honest employment," and with it all often go many hard words for the men in power.

Nothing is said about the employer who grows old before his time in a vain attempt to get frowsy ne'er-do-wells to do intelligent work; and his long, patient striving with "help" that does nothing but loaf when his back is turned. In every store and factory there is a constant weeding-out process going on. The employer is continually sending away "help" that have shown their incapacity to further the interests of the business, and others are being taken on.

No matter how good times are, this sorting continues: only if times are hard and work is scarce, the sorting is done finer—but out and forever out the incompetent and unworthy go. It is the survival of the fittest. Self-interest prompts every employer to keep the best—those who can carry a message to Garcia.

I know one man of really brilliant parts who has not the ability to manage a business of his own, and yet who is

175

absolutely worthless to anyone else, because he carries with him constantly the insane suspicion that his employer is oppressing, or intending to oppress, him. He cannot give orders; and he will not receive them. Should a message be given him to take to Garcia, his answer would probably be, "Take it yourself!"

Tonight this man walks the streets looking for work, the wind whistling through his threadbare coat. No one who knows him dare employ him, for he is a regular firebrand of discontent. He is impervious to reason, and the only thing that can impress him is the toe of a thick-soled Number Nine boot.

Of course I know that one so morally deformed is no less to be pitied than a physical cripple; but in our pitying let us drop a tear, too, for the men who are striving to carry on a great enterprise, whose working hours are not limited by the whistle, and whose hair is fast turning white through the struggle to hold in line dowdy indifference, slipshod imbecility, and the heartless ingratitude which, but for their enterprise, would be both hungry and homeless.

Have I put the matter too strongly? Possibly I have; but when all the world has gone a-slumming I wish to speak a word of sympathy for the man who succeeds—the man who, against great odds, has directed the efforts of others, and having succeeded, finds there's nothing in it: nothing but bare board and clothes. I have carried a dinner-pail and worked for day's wages, and I have also been an employer of labor, and I know there is something to be said on both sides. There is no excellence, per se, in poverty; rags are no recommendation; and all employers are not rapacious and high-handed, any more than all poor men are virtuous.

My heart goes out to the man who does his work when the "boss" is away, as well as when he is at home. And the man who, when given a letter for Garcia, quietly takes the missive, without asking any idiotic questions, and with no lurking intention of chucking it into the nearest sewer, or of doing aught else but deliver it, never gets "laid off," nor has to go on a strike for higher wages. Civilization is one long, anxious search for just such individuals. Anything such a man asks shall be granted. His kind is so rare that no employer can afford to let him go. He is wanted in every city, town and village—in every office, shop, store, and factory.

The world cries out for such: he is needed, and needed badly—the man who can carry **A MESSAGE TO GARCIA.**

Andrew Summers Rowan (April 23, 1857-January 10, 1943) was a West Point cadet and American Army officer who served in the Spanish American War, the Philippine War, and the Moro Rebellion, and became famous for delivering a message from President McKinley to General Garcia in Cuba.

Chapter 12—The Playbook of

Elbert Hubbard

You may not know of Elbert Hubbard, pictured on the right, but I could not have written this book if he had not existed. Besides being the author of *A Message to Garcia* and many other books and publications, he was a philosopher, lecturer, salesman, inventor, farmer, editor, and well-known personality during his time. Most of all, for my and your purposes, he was a highly successful businessman.

His business, founded in 1895, in the village of East Aurora, New York, near Buffalo, New York, was a community of highly-skilled craftsmen and artists whom he titled *The Roycrofters*, a name originally reserved in England only for those craftsmen skilled enough to produce their fine wares for the king.

Among them were printers, furniture makers, metalsmiths, leathersmiths, and bookbinders; and together their reformist community, often referred to as *The Roycroft Movement,* owing to the work and philosophy of the group, had a strong influence on the development of American architecture and design in the early 20th century.

For our concern, however, Hubbard, much like all of us, was always looking for people that were willing to work hard and make a contribution to his company. Employing over 500 people, *The Roycrofters* quickly grew to become the major business enterprise in East Aurora, attracting thousands of visitors every year from all parts of the world, most especially for their high-quality furniture. They were a leading producer of Mission Style products.

Today it is not unusual to see products with a logo of the company printed somewhere on the product. But that very practice was simply taboo in the early 20th century. Nobody did it. It was just considered shameful bad practice.

But not for Hubbard. In fact, he was one of the first persons to develop the concept of what we routinely call today "product branding," one of the most significant revolutionary business practices of his day that made Hubbard such a controversial figure.

Along with that, though, he also had his own style of dress: he wore a floppy hat, flannel shirt, and cowboy boots just about every where he went. Why? Because he knew the importance of separating oneself from the crowd, both in product identity and personally. The benefit to Hubbard was that it was his style of dress that made him so easily recognizable, even amid the crowded streets and hustle and bustle of New York City. When he arrived in that city for business, everybody quickly knew it.

Elbert Green Hubbard was born in 1856 in Bloomington, Illinois, to Silas Hubbard, a country doctor, and Juliana Frances Read. One of six children, Elbert had one older sister and brother, and three younger sisters. He spent much of his childhood playing outdoors and riding horses, the latter of which became one of his greatest enjoyments. For the record, though, he really didn't show much interest in school, and was actually considered a troublemaker by some.

Regardless, a major part of Hubbard's philosophy was his belief in education, but not just classroom book learning. He strongly believed that a sound education also had to include learning a trade or developing a skill that was needed in everyday life. And he demonstrated this belief in his business by offering that type of training to the young people who came to work for him. In whichever of his shops they preferred to work, they were taught the trade by the highly-skilled artisans already there. In addition, however, they had the opportunity during their evenings and weekends to learn from the many educated and famous visitors who came to visit *The Roycrofters*. It was a basic belief of Hubbard that an educated person was one who knows how to produce more than he consumes.

Hubbard began his business career as a door-to-door salesman selling soap for the Larkin Soap Company. And it was he who originally came up with the idea of what salespeople today refer to as "The Puppy Dog Close." In his case, though, he simply called it "Leave on Trial." He would leave his product with the woman of the house and allow her to use it without charge for a short while, making it clear to each that, were they not happy with it, they would not have to pay for it when he returned a few days later. He also made it clear to them that he believed in providing quality products for the money people had to pay for them. His technique took many of his prospects by complete surprise, and he sold a ton of soap that way. Understandably, he quickly moved up in the company.

But Hubbard's vision and ambition far superseded the life of a door-to-door salesman. So he soon cashed in his stock, and took the money to begin developing his own business; and that's what eventually became known as *The Roycrofters* in East Aurora.

But he certainly didn't stop there. Being a rather astute student of human nature (today we call it psychology), his successes and insights soon led him to write, teach, and lecture on the subject of successful business practices to great length. He made no bones about his not having had any extensive formal schooling, but made it clear that he did consider himself, as he used to say, a graduate of the "University of Hard Knocks".

Many have called Hubbard a philosopher, but in that same home-spun style for which Will Rogers would later become famous. That is, most of his sayings were along the lines of common-sense messages, often laced with incisive quips of humor, and many of his quotes were insights about achieving success.

Here are a few of my favorites:

- How many a man has thrown up his hands at a time when a little more effort, a little more patience, would have achieved success?
- Get happiness out of your work, or you may never know what happiness is.
- Life is just one damn thing after another.
- Don't take life too seriously. You'll never get out of it

alive!

- One machine can do the work of fifty ordinary men; but no machine can do the work of one extraordinary man.
- Never explain—your friends do not need it, and your enemies will not believe you, anyway.
- The object of teaching a child is to enable him to get along without a teacher.
- The greatest mistake you can make in life is to be continually fearing you will make one.
- It does not take much strength to do things, but it requires a great deal of strength to decide what to do.
- There is no failure except in no longer trying.
- The world is moving so fast these days that the man who says it can't be done is generally interrupted by someone doing it.
- The line between failure and success is so fine...that we are often on the line and do not know it.

As an adjunct to Hubbard's business success with *The Roycrofters*, he also edited and published two magazines, *The Philistine* and *The Fra*. At its height, although *The Philistine* had over 200,000 monthly subscribers, because he chose to bind it in brown butcher paper, and because it was so full of satire and plain talk, some people considered him an anarchist and revolutionary. But at the same time, others esteemed him a genius and a great thinker.

To be sure, Hubbard was a prolific writer of pamphlets and books. Some of his book titles include:

- *Health and Wealth*
- *The Book of Business*
- *Get Out or Get in Line*
- *Elbert Hubbard's Scrapbook: Containing the Inspired and Inspiring Selections, Gathered During a Lifetime of Discriminating Reading for His Own Use by Elbert Hubbard*
- *The Philosophy of Elbert Hubbard*
- *The Dogs of War*
- *Love, Life, and Work: How to Attain the Highest Possible Happiness for One's Self with the Least Possible Harm to Others*
- *So Here Cometh White Hyacinths: Being a Book of the Heart Wherein Is an Attempt to Body Forth Ideas and Ideals for the Betterment of Men*
- *Health and Wealth*

- *The Science of Advertising*
- *The Romance of Business*
- *Time and Chance: A Romance and a History; Being the Story of the Life of a Man*
- *Essay on Silence.* Hubbard loved to joke, as this was a book that contained only blank pages.

On top of all of this, he also wrote a series of 182 biographies of famous persons of history, and of many of his own contemporaries, under the series title, "Little Journeys to Homes of the Great."

As Hubbard's reputation grew, his demand as a lecturer expanded throughout the country and abroad, such that there was no more sought-after lecturer than he from 1900 to 1915. He easily drew two to three thousand people at a lecture, and found himself speaking in places like New York City, Chicago, Boston, Minneapolis, Cincinnati, Omaha, Denver, Spokane, Seattle, Portland, San Francisco, Los Angeles, and Philadelphia.

In Philadelphia, in fact, the practice at the Clover Club was to shout down the speaker, to make him leave the stage. But the audience there quickly learned that they were simply no match for Elbert Hubbard. He gave every bit as good as he got! And, unlike

many others on the lecture circuit back then, there was no subject
that he was not willing to speak on. Believe it or not, in 1908, he
was actually nothing less than the keynote speaker at the annual
meeting of *The Society in Dedham for Apprehending Horse
Thieves.* If that doesn't impress you readers, I really don't know
what will.

Although normally very upbeat, energetic, and genuinely
positive, there was one thing that he absolutely hated, and that was
cigarette smoking. Paddling wholly against the tide on this one, he
not only argued that it was a waste of time, but that it was also
awful for your health. Hmph, guess he was ahead of his time on
that one too, wasn't he?

Soon enough, owing to Hubbard's by-now widespread
fame, people from all over America and Europe came to East
Aurora to visit him, hundreds of people every year. The
Roycrofters was a solid, but relatively simple community,
comprised of a hotel, print shop, barns, cottages, storage buildings,
and woodworking shops. Even so, the long list of prestigious
visitors included politicians, industrial magnates, writers, actors,
royalty, and sports figures; people like: Clara Barton, Carrie Jacobs
Bond, Stephen Crane, Clarence Darrow, Thomas Edison, Henry
Ford, Ben Greet, E.H. Harriman, Frank Keenan, Edwin Markham,

Theodore Roosevelt, Carl Sandburg, William H. Taft, Elizabeth Towne, Fred Underwood, Booker T. Washington, Harry Weinberger, Woodrow Wilson, and Ed Wynne, to name only a few of the many visitors.

In those days, of course, most people traveled by train, horse, or wagon. Very few commoners could afford to come by car. And what they found at *The Roycrofters* was a self-contained community of hard-working, highly-accomplished artisans, laborers, skilled tradesmen, inventors, and entrepreneurs. What they did not find were any loafers.

In no time, throngs of hopeful participants and potential employees also began to arrive, looking to become a part of this thriving industrious community. But it was not unusual to have someone arrive on the morning train, interview with Hubbard or one of his managers, only to find themselves taken to the train station for the "4 o'clock" and given a ticket to Buffalo, after being told they were just not going to "work out."

Our story of Elbert Hubbard ends rather tragically, unfortunately, on May 7, 1915. On the first of that month, he and his wife Alice boarded the luxury passenger ship the *Lusitania* in New York City. They were sailing to Ireland and then on to Europe to report on the First World War, and he hoped to

188

land an interview with Kaiser Wilhelm II. However, on that fateful May 7, 1915, the *Lusitania* was torpedoed by a German submarine, and sunk into the depths of the Atlantic. Both Hubbard and his wife went down with the ship along with 1,195 other passengers.

I've included this special chapter on Elbert Hubbard simply because I hope that you will find him as wise in the ways of business, and as inspirational a leader as I have found him to be. I was introduced to the man through his writing of *A Message to Garcia*, and have since found his work, his philosophy, his writings, his leadership principles, and his very life to be an entire business education in itself. My hope is that you too might consider looking a little closer at the man and see if what he has done, and what he has written, might also be a help and an inspiration to you in your business.

If it helps, I might suggest a reading of *Elbert Hubbard of East Aurora,* by Felix Shay, a man who worked for Hubbard for over thirty years. I found it particularly significant that the foreword to that book was written by Hubbard's friend Henry Ford, a man not in the habit of endorsing other people. Ford's willingness to do so, however, is just one example of the kind of people who admired and respected Elbert Hubbard. If time is in short supply for you, perhaps I can then suggest a viewing of the

PBS special *Elbert Hubbard: An American Original*, available on the internet, YouTube, at: http://video.pbs.org/video/1336444205/.

Chapter 13—A Message to Garcia...
...IS a Message to Leaders Today!

You might be wondering how something from so long ago could be relevant to the success of business in the society and world that we live in today.

Please take a closer look.

The lesson that is extracted from *A Message to Garcia* is a lesson that will stand the test of time for all eternity. It is a powerful message that is relevant for any and every age, in business or otherwise. It doesn't really matter what the nature of a project is, what the mission is. Nor is it all that important what tools or sophisticated technology are available.

Rather, the most important element that will determine the success or failure of any project or task or venture is simply the way a worker approaches that task. We're talking about his or her commitment, that regrettably rare attitude of, "I'll get it done!" "I have a job to do, get out of my way; I've been given an assignment!" "I'm an honest man, and I'm going to give an honest day's work!"

And that is precisely the eternal lesson that *A Message to Garcia* delivers; a message of no-holds-barred commitment to a task.

To be sure, the significance of *A Message to Garcia* is actually twofold, and both have to do with timing.

The first was the timelessness of the story—e.g., how one man can impact events that change the world by following through with individual effort on a task he is given. The second is simply that the impact of the story has much to do with the era during which it was written.

The world was changing very rapidly at the beginning of the 20th century. With the onset of the Industrial Age, the "modern era" that was being ushered in required an efficient method of providing instruction to the masses. Besides giving speeches to necessarily limited gatherings directly, the only other method available to reach greater, more widely distributed audiences was via the distribution of printed material. Limited as that may seem today in our 21st century, back then it was the only other way to get information out into the world.

The author, Elbert Hubbard, makes mention of how he had published it on a whim. He needed to fill a little extra space in his popular newspaper, *The Philistine*, of which he was the publisher and editor. We also saw how, in just a few days, he started getting more and more orders for that particular edition, until the New York Central Railroad requested a quote on 100,000 copies of the story in pamphlet form. In 1899, the railroad business was the ultimate "state of the art" business. That request was huge. And you recall how the request for the story multiplied exponentially from there, to where *A Message to Garcia* became, and likely still is, the most published item ever produced during the lifetime of the author.

Think about it a minute. Why did so many companies, armies, and other institutions latch on to this story and distribute it throughout their organizations? They must have had a very important reason.

I'd say the answer is fairly obvious. The decision-makers who had it distributed were looking for an effective way to teach their employees or military service personnel or other subordinates what was expected of them.

Remember that, at the turn of the 20th century, very few people had more than a grade-school education, and some did not even have that. The majority had been raised on small farms and weren't used to working for other people. The world was changing, and business leaders and managers needed a way to teach workers the skills necessary for the success of an ongoing enterprise.

When Elbert Hubbard published *A Message to Garcia* in 1899, he had no idea what kind of reaction his story would create. What he did not realize was that he had written a story that had universal appeal, one that could be used by every organization and company to provide instruction and motivation to its personnel. As a man of business, Elbert Hubbard readily understood the need to train employees, but I doubt that he himself even recognized at first how his little story was going to have such a powerful impact on that particular universal need.

The mass distribution of *A Message to Garcia* was a historical phenomenon that cannot be underestimated. At the same time, however, if the goal in writing and distributing it was to use it as an instructional and motivational learning opportunity, we really don't have any record of whether or not that attempt was successful.

I suspect that its impact was limited, despite the power that the story holds. I say that because I doubt very much that the men who decided to have this story distributed within their domains gave any instruction on how it could be used. They probably simply gave an order to have it distributed and to have their people read it.

There are two problems with this approach. The first one is that you don't know if someone has learned anything from simply reading a given piece. It's essential that they be *asked* what they learned. You have to test them.

The second problem is that it was not made clear what they expected them to learn. It makes pretty clear sense that what all of the decision-makers intended to teach was the importance of their subordinates adopting the mindset, the personally responsible character trait possessed by Rowan. I call this Creative Initiative. But I'm not convinced that that is a trait that can be taught so easily.

That's okay. Because what I know you can do is identify it within people, and use this information to great advantage in moving your business down the road to success.

In the following material, I will show you how I myself used *A Message to Garcia* with my own employees, not only to help me determine whom I should hire in the first place, but also to instruct those that I had determined were a good fit for us. And I think you'll readily see that you too can do exactly what I did, and I'm sure you will meet with the same success. There are few things sweeter than having all of your employees on the same page. If you can do that, I think you'll find that success is just waiting at the top of that mountain for you.

Let's take a look.

Chapter 14—Searching for Rowan:
Creative Initiative!

In *A Message to Garcia,* the main character, Andrew Summers Rowan, a Lieutenant in the United States Army, is given a supremely important assignment by President McKinley. He was to deliver a critical message to a single man whom no one could find, hidden away in the depths of a jungle that only very few could navigate or traverse.

And yet Rowan did it. It took him three arduous weeks. But he did it.

We never get to see the details of his trek. We never learn of the obstacles in his path. We only know today of his success. So it makes one wonder, doesn't it, what were the character traits that Rowan had that enabled him to be a success, even in the face of such an incredible challenge?

I'm sure his story was so widely distributed because they are these same character traits that were so sought after by those who distributed his story. Like me, probably like you too, they wanted their people to learn from the actions of Andrew Summers Rowan, and to adopt the same "get-the-job-done-at-all-costs" attitude that he had.

So what are the Rowan Traits? Who has them? And how do you know?

In one sense, it's all really very simple. Rowan understood the assignment, and then turned about and delivered it. He didn't complain about it, he didn't whine about it, he didn't even brag about it. He just went out and got it done.

When you, as an employer, or even as a manager, come across someone like that, you know right away that you've found a person who can be successful regardless of the setting they find themselves in, and practically regardless of the assignment you give them.

Let's say they are a technical person, but you need a marketing answer. It's really not important whether they have a technical background or a marketing background. What's important is that they have the sort of character that is going to require them, as a matter of self worth, to do all that is necessary to accomplish the task. They will *learn* how to be a marketer.

Today, with thousands of college graduates with numerous degrees, you would think that Rowan traits would be easy to find in employees. Unfortunately, that's just not the case, so I'd advise you not to expect it. It has been my experience that college doesn't prepare the individual to really seize initiative. Rather it teaches him or her to work within a complex bureaucracy that often delivers rewards, but rewards that are based upon results that are not necessarily relevant to the overall success of the company. In fact, in some cases, they only learn how to get by! They learn to what level they need to advance, but then go no further!

But hang on here. Don't get me wrong. There's no question in my mind about the immense value of an accomplished academic background, the comfortable grasp of concepts and information intrinsic to one's chosen field. I also greatly applaud academia's continual emphasis and training in a student's ability to educate oneself further in any subject or matter of relevant concern in one's field—or in any field, for that matter! And most university programs, as well as all corporate internship programs, go a long way toward helping students and new employees develop and hone the skills required to work together with diverse groups and disciplines in a collaborative environment.

However, I think it's important to be clear here. Being successful academically does not necessarily mean one is going to be successful in other areas.

Many people who graduate from a university learn to blend in with the crowd rather than stand out. And yet, most people who succeed, almost always overcoming significant obstacles, are going to stand out from the crowd in some way or another. Often their success is owed more to a sore thumb than a pretty one.

Structured environments can also stifle individual expression, and yet individual expression is a basic Rowan Trait! To be sure, there are many times too when the often overly-gregarious nature of such a person can appear to be on the verge of being offensive.

Given all of that, I have to tell you that I would much rather have someone who genuinely wants the job, and gives it a hundred per cent—but maybe has only an average SAT score—than someone who has a high-flying SAT score, but is not fully engaged in an assignment that supports my company. Unfortunately, as you have likely already seen, that's the guy who's willing to do whatever it takes to get the paycheck, but not what it takes to get the job done.

This seems to happen a lot in the academic world. It's a world where people are geared toward achieving high marks, passing courses with excellent grades, getting that cherished diploma, but too often not necessarily obtaining and internalizing the innate skills that will be required for them to be successful in their field.

And just to be clear, having Rowan traits is certainly not in any way contingent on one's gender, race, creed, handicap, political affiliation, or anything else. All types of people are capable of having Rowan traits! It is quite simply a matter of one's willingness to take those steps necessary to succeed.

A Rowan is Not Reckless

Someone who is really a Rowan doesn't look at the steps he takes as being a risk. On the contrary, he looks at them as necessities, as the things that simply need to be done to successfully accomplish a task.

You might say, "Well, isn't that really a risk-taker?"

A Rowan doesn't see it that way. In fact, she thinks it is more of a risk *not* to act, than it is to act. Her mind and heart tell her that she has an *obligation* to act, and, if she doesn't, then she feels that anything that goes wrong will be her fault. Her concern is not that someone else might point the finger at her and say it was her fault. She really doesn't care about that so much. It's quite the opposite. Her primary concern, what's intrinsic to her character, is that she *cannot let a necessary action go undone.* Above all else, she feels personal responsibility to fully complete the task.

Allow me to pause a moment here and clear up a common

misunderstanding held by many employers and managers. Many think that a Rowan type individual is someone who is reckless. I'd have to disagree. That's simply not the case. He has to weigh all things, consider all opportunities to the best of his abilities, gather intelligence, and survey his contemporaries to determine what they think is the right course of action. Only then does he act.

It is not about kicking the door down and then finding out it's the wrong building! It is about checking the address three times…because you are a Rowan and you don't want to make a mistake. It's about checking the search warrant three times… because you are a Rowan. It is about checking the addresses of the houses on either side of you…because you are a Rowan. It is about opening up the mail box and checking the addresses on that mail to make sure that it is the right house, and then walking down to the end of the street and looking at the street sign to make sure you are on the right street. That's a Rowan! He doesn't just go up and kick the door in.

That's the difference between a Rowan and someone who is just reckless and irresponsible. A Rowan is not reckless. He's not irresponsible and, you know what? He surely might be thought of as being aggressive. However, in reality, his actions have little to do with aggression. And, if he appears to be a risk-taker, his perspective on risk is a lot different than the norm. Risk-takers can be foolishly careless. A Rowan is not. *His diligent preparation is his safety net.* But his very perception of risk is unique. The "risk" to a Rowan is the risk of *not* acting, or of taking the *wrong* action. It is never the risk of taking action in itself.

That's a concept that is very difficult for a lot of people to embrace.

The Traits of a Rowan

So what do Rowans do that so many others don't do?

Focus: For one thing, they are able to focus their attention on details. That focus allows them to see the big picture much more clearly, much more thoroughly, than most. They rarely miss anything important to the task. Without question, the ability to focus is a major Rowan trait.

Perseverance: Most people who are Rowans have failed more times than they have succeeded. But they have also tried many more times than the average. That's big. I would rather have someone try three different ways to get the door open, fail twice, and get the door open on the third try, than someone who doesn't even try to open the door. Their focused intent, the choices they make, are to be able to accomplish the goal.

Right or wrong, Rowans are going to make mistakes. The only way you don't make mistakes is by not doing anything. And it is so disheartening to find so many people who choose that as the person they will be.

"I won't make any mistakes!"

"I won't fail!"

"I won't have anything go wrong, because I won't take any chances."

A Rowan thinks just the opposite.

She thinks, "I should have done that."

"It's my fault that I didn't take care of it!"

"I won't let something like that happen again!"

"I'll stand up! And I would rather get in trouble than not do what I think is right!"

A Rowan doesn't act impulsively or recklessly. They have to do the research; they have to do the work behind the project. Nobody would give a damn about Rowan if he ultimately failed. Elbert Hubbard wouldn't have written a story about him. Rowan's are successful, and they are successful, not just because they react, but because they act based upon reasoned intelligence, reasoned processes.

Research Oriented: They ask lots of questions, and gather skills by gathering other people to help support their decision. If you ask a Rowan how he actually came to his decision, he'll probably confide that it was not his decision alone. He'll probably also tell you that he surveyed the situation, he asked what was available, and he inventoried what he had. And, only after all of that, will he tell you that, for him, there was really only one conclusion, only one path that he was able to identify that would be successful.

The problem is that so many people who have Rowan skills aren't even looking to be successful. They are only interested in getting a check, and getting out on time or getting off work early. Maybe, if they're lucky, they might even get credit for something they didn't do.

I can tell you, though, a Rowan character is not programmed that way at all. She is only interested in successfully accomplishing the goal. And, if she falls down, she picks herself back up and keeps on going. She doesn't fall down, and then get caught up in so much overwhelming fear at her falling that she becomes afraid to get back up. Perseverance is an essential Rowan characteristic.

Let's be clear, though. Young Rowans in a classroom can often become a challenge. It depends a lot upon the structure of the

was sentenced to twenty years in Spandau Prison in West Berlin, not least of all for using slave labor in his factories. By all accounts, he was a willing participant in the highest levels of some of the most atrocious actions in history. At the same time, just to make the point, he was probably one of the most Rowan-like characters in Nazi, Germany. It might be said that Speer was more Rowan-like than Rowan himself in terms of his organizational skills and his willingness to take on responsibility, not to mention his ability to move through difficult processes and get things done.

At the end of WWII, when Germany was losing the war, and had by then had all their cities bombed out, the production of armaments was higher that at any other period of the war. And that was when they were on the verge of collapse!

How could this be? It was because Speer was behind it. It didn't matter to him why he was doing it. He had a job to do, and he was figuring out a way to do it.

Our space program is another example of how Rowan traits can be used for good or bad. Wernher Von Braun (1912-1977) was a technocrat. When he was working for the Germans, he was building the best rockets possible, and he didn't care how or why. He was on a mission; he was another Rowan. When the war ended, he came to work for the United States. The next thing you know, he was developing *our* rocket program. The same rockets used for our space program were also used for our defense program, using the exact same technology.

So here's a guy who was on the worst side of history and on the best side of history in one lifetime. Why was he able to have such overwhelming success? Because he had those same qualities that we are talking about—Creative Initiative.

So whether they're good or bad, that doesn't often even come into the picture. The best Rowans are so into getting the job done, they may not even have a perspective on its overall affect. Their primary perspective is how to accomplish it. One week Von Braun is wearing a swastika and the next week he is waving the American flag. He is a strong example of a Rowan.

Those same qualities sometimes don't become as apparent when the individual stays on the same team. It sometimes happens that their dedication and compulsive need to succeed become shrouded in their environment. When you see someone who can move from one side of an issue to another, and still remain just as effective and successful, you can be reasonably sure you're looking at a Rowan-type character. They have become a technocrat. And when they become a technocrat about leadership, look out! You have to get out of their way.

That is the key word. That's the thing with someone who is

a technocrat. In this photo, we see Wernher Von Braun with President John F. Kennedy, following the President's challenge to travel to the moon. It was practical for Wernher Von Braun to transfer to the United States missile program. He could have just as easily headed up the missile program for the Soviet Union. Although he surrendered to the United States, trust me, if he had been captured by the Russians, he would have run their program instead. And you know what? He probably would have been just as content.

It was nice for Von Braun to be able to look back and state that he made a decision to come to the United States because he didn't want to ally himself with the side that didn't believe in God. On the other hand, if he had been captured by the Russians, I am sure that he would have had an equally eloquent manner of explaining why he wanted to work for them. Because, for a

Wernher Von Braun, what it was going to be about for him was the work itself, no matter what the policies were for which he was working.

Those are the key traits of a Rowan—the ability to assume individual responsibility, to focus, to persevere, and to seek creative solutions to complicated problems.

Chapter 15—How to Know One
When You See One

As a business owner, I was always looking for the best people I could find. I used employment offices, community referral agencies, professional magazines, newspapers, and word-of-mouth to locate potential employees.

Like many companies, seventy percent of the people I hire are high school graduates, twenty-five percent have some college, and five percent are college graduates. I was always surprised at the diverse experiences that many of my employees had.

I know from experience it is not easy to identify a Rowan. The most important attribute to have when looking for exceptional employees is to be a person who has acquired the skill of self-discipline and personal responsibility. In other words—"It takes one to know one."

You have to be a Rowan-type person yourself in order to maintain a successful business. Anyone can start a business—that's why so many people go out of business and fail! Maintaining a successful business requires a Rowan-type character with those attributes of perseverance, ability to focus, creative problem-solving skills, and the acceptance of responsibility to see that goals are completed. This skill set helps you both identify a Rowan, and manage one.

When you are first starting a business, it's very hard to be successful if those first critical tasks are not properly executed. You need some Rowans working for you. If not, you yourself have to *BE* them. *You* have to be the person who is in the lead position. You must be the one who is setting the pace for everyone else, for how things need to be done. And I can assure you, it is much easier to achieve this when you have an employee who you can depend on to accomplish critical tasks that are important to the start-up of your business.

Enhancing Your Own Rowan Skills

What do you do if you don't consider yourself a Rowan?

Today anyone with the right mindset can certainly be Rowan-type, and can consequently be in pretty high demand just about anywhere.

Some of the skills that are part of the Rowan character today are available through the technology that has been invented. The computer has made it possible for a lot of people, who have the desire but are lacking a few of the organizational skills, to become more of a Rowan-type character.

For instance, there's the calendar that you can maintain on your phone and iPad, or your computer with its alarms and reminders and so forth. This is a wonderful aid for some people who perhaps get distracted or lose tract of what they need to do.

These kinds of tools have been around and available to business people for years, probably for a couple of centuries. But not like today! Nobody today has to walk around with a printed calendar or maybe a phone book under their arm. Probably a good thing, right? Today you can have everything at the touch of your fingers, and have it remind you about things that, in their absence, you and I probably wouldn't remember in a thousand years! And, to boot, we can share the stuff with whomever we choose.

This is basic, I know! But when taken full advantage of, today's technology can really boost the productivity and creativity of a whole bunch more people who have the desire to perform like a Rowan, but might be otherwise lacking a few simple tools to actually pull it off. Now, finally, they've got pretty much all the tools they need to complement their ambition to succeed. They can focus on the task a lot better than ever before in business history.

Here's a caution, though.

Sometimes people who aspire to be a Rowan can overdo it with too much technology. They spend so much time keeping track of everything that they forget to actually execute! But, for the most part, the technology enhances the Rowan-type individual.

When you think about it, isn't a computer a type of Rowan in a way?

One big difference, however, is the computer doesn't act independently, and that is the key characteristic of a Rowan. It only assists with recognizing and attacking some of the tactical things that are necessary to a strategic goal, without having to be taken by the hand and shown the way. It is a tool that can enhance, as well as distract, if you don't use it the right way. As you well know, it can just as easily be used to play solitaire as to review the latest report that was sent over to you.

Technology is only a tool to assist us in achieving our business goals; it requires people with Rowan character, that all-important "Creative Initiative", to actually make it happen. Elbert Hubbard was right when he said, "One machine can do the work of fifty ordinary men. No machine can do the work of one extraordinary man."

The Rowans I have encountered are unassuming and understated, so they are difficult to identify during a normal interview.

Identifying a Rowan

As you probably already know, interviewing a potential employee, or an accountant, an attorney, or any other potential business partner, can be tricky at best. I have read some outstanding resumes in my time, and some others of them were very likely among the best fiction ever written.

Today, of course, you have to be very careful about what you ask someone during a job interview. There have certainly been plenty of times when I would like to have asked a question, but have hesitated because I didn't want it to be misinterpreted.

Once hired, you have to get to know your employees as much as possible in order to effectively take advantage of their skills and abilities. To do this, I have developed a two-step system that I use with new employees that involves: 1) an informal group event, and 2) an assignment which I call my "Rowan Exercise," using *A Message to Garcia*.

The Rowan Exercise was always particularly telling. It went something like this.

At the initial interview, if I was genuinely interested in a prospect, but maybe wasn't completely sold yet, I'd give them a copy of *A Message to Garcia.* I'd ask them to take it home, read it through, and then write out their impressions of what it said to them.

Some interviewees would start asking questions.

"Well, when do you want it back?"

"Whenever you get it completed," I'd tell them.

"Soooo, why do you want me to do this?"

"Oh, it's just part of the interview process for all of our employees. You don't HAVE to do it!"

"Well, what's it about?

"That's what you'll learn when you read it."

"Okay, so what do you want? A sentence or two? A couple of paragraphs? Pages? What do you need?"

"That's up to you," I'd tell them.

And I was always amazed at how much I'd learn about each applicant just from the way they handled this one little exercise. Some would come back in a few days with a couple of sentences written out. Others would return with several pages of rather complex reflections. Some would return the exercise to me the next day, but others maybe a week or two later. Of course, there were always those who just never quite got around to doing it at all. I learned something about each one that I don't think I could have readily assessed any other way, simply by how they handled this one exercise.

Can you guess what the Rowan-types usually did?

They'd invariably return it the very next day, usually typed out very neatly, and generally filling at least a full page, if not several pages. It's really sweet when your heart starts skipping a beat for all the right reasons.

I want to emphasize that it's absolutely a strategic decision to seek out a Rowan-type person. It is something that you have to make a priority, and develop a skill at identifying them. It has taken me many years in refining this skill myself. I guess my kids might say I practiced on them. Maybe so. Here's a case in point.

The Bike

My son had a bike stolen. It was parked right in front of the house. He was about seven or eight years old at the time and, like many young children, that bike was his entire world. So I told him and his brothers that we were going to find out where it went.

Not surprisingly, they were a little skeptical.

"You gotta be kiddin', Dad. How are we ever gonna find a stolen bike? That thing might be in a whole other city by now!"

They wanted to know *how* we were going to find it. And

they were not brimming over with confidence that it could be done.

But I reasoned to myself that, because the bike was just sitting out in the yard when it was taken, the theft was very likely a simple matter of ease of opportunity. Probably the temptation, at least to another kid in the habit of stealing stuff, was very likely too much to resist. And that itself also suggested to me that the thief was much more likely to be living in our own neighborhood than belonging to some statewide bicycle theft ring that was cruising around after dark with a clandestine moving van making his black market fortune by peddling…well, peddles n' stuff.

Anyway, I told the boys to get in the car.

Then we started driving slowly around our neighborhood. To none of our surprise, we didn't see it.

So then we drove around the whole subdivision. We looked in the parks, we slowed down when we went by people's houses, and we always scrutinized any open garages.

Still, we didn't see it.

The next day, however, we did the same thing. Of course, my sons were fairly convinced I had lost my mind this time. But, being dutiful, obedient sons, they played along, humoring ol' Dad. Nice of them, right? But, in my own mind, I suspected that, after a day or two, the thief kid was likely to lower his guard, and just might be a little careless with where he was hiding his stolen goods.

The third day, after church, we drove through a neighboring subdivision which was about three quarters of a mile away from our house. We did exactly the same thing we'd been doing for the two days before. We drove slow, we scrutinized open garages, and we closely zoomed in on every bicycle we came across…and even parts of a bicycle.

And then, BINGO!

We saw the distinctive handle bars of his bike sticking up out of the back of a truck. I think it blew the boys out of the water! For my part, I'll have to admit that it also brought a pretty cool smile to my face.

So we stopped, we got out, and we looked in the garage. That garage was full of bikes, all kinds of bikes! Maybe this kid was running a statewide operation! It looked like a bicycle chop shop!

We went to the front door of the house and knocked.

"You got our bike in your truck."

The man acted real cool, like he'd had to deal with these kinds of confrontations for years now. Quickly made me realize who was the brains of the outfit.

Acting a little surprised, he said, "Oh, my son found it, and didn't think you wanted it, and thought you were going to get rid of it. We were going to give it to a cousin of ours that lives in another town."

Then his son too showed up at the door, with a calm as practiced as his dad's. He was a teenager, a lot older than my kid. There was no question that they had stolen the bike. If not, the kid's "cousin" was about to be the recipient of a couple dozen bikes; he'd get to take his pick! It was clear as a springtime stream that they had stolen every one of those bikes.

I live in a pretty nice neighborhood, so I called the police. "Oh, we know them," they told us. Hmph.

At any rate, hopefully the whole exercise not only got my son back in the saddle of his beloved bike again, but did so with the boys learning a valuable life lesson at the same time. More importantly still, I hoped that my confidence, problem-solving, and persistence, would offer a memorable example of some of the traits that I knew would serve them well into their future.

As I write this, I'm pretty sure that I won't have to worry about any of my kids actually reading it. After all, I'm their dad. They've heard about these same principles for about twenty years now, mostly at the kitchen table, so I'm fairly confident that they don't really need to read it. By now, they all know it! All four of them, I'm very proud to say.

After this little incident, and quite a few more like it, they know that you don't give up until you find what you need. Three days of looking for a bike? You got to figure the bike is pretty well gone. At the same time, however, you know darn well that it didn't evaporate.

We might not have found the bike. There are a lot of things that get stolen that you never ever find, right? But we would certainly never have found it if we never went out and looked for it! That was a lesson for a young boy about how not to give up, and how to keep at something until you achieve whatever you're after.

It's the same principle with looking for Rowan-type employees. I will tell you with certainty that you will never find a Rowan if you don't make the effort to look for him. What I mean here is simply that a company's success or failure in finding solid Rowan-type employees is all contingent on whether or not the owner or manager or supervisor is actually out there, with eyes and ears on the alert, genuinely seeking just such a person as a priority. This isn't fly-by-the-seat-of-your-pants hiring here. It's just way too important a task. On the contrary, engaging in an ongoing diligent search for the Rowans in your hiring waiting room, or among those already in your company, must become a strategic decision!

And, to be sure, this does not only apply to hiring or to promoting from within, or even just to your own employees. If you need to hire an attorney, as we all do at some point, or an accountant, or any other outside contract associate, may I urge you to keep your eyes equally wide open for that same kind of person who, regardless of the challenges that may arise in his or her path, will deliver that message to Garcia.

Chapter 16—How to Manage a "Rowan"

Supervision is almost an art form when you are dealing with a Rowan-type character. In this section, let's take a look at various aspects of supervision that are specific to Rowan-type employees, as well as some general aspects of supervision as well.

Different people require different levels of supervision. If you've ever supervised more than one person, you already know this well. Some people require almost ongoing direction, and others need only minimal direction. In addition, the amount of supervision a person may require depends on the task assigned. Too little supervision, or too much supervision, can both create problems.

If you are going to maximize the benefit of having a Rowan as an employee, there are several aspects of supervision you need to be aware of. Remember that Rowans can indeed work independently, but can just as efficiently work as part of a team. They can be a leader, or they can be a follower. It really depends on how they size up what is needed to get the job done.

Take a look at the movie *The Untouchables*, starring Kevin

Costner, Sean Connery, and Robert DeNiro. It's a good example of how a person with Rowan-type skills can function both independently and as a team player. In the movie, Al Capone, played by Robert De Niro, has a conversation about baseball. He talks about it being a team sport. But, he says, when a man stands behind the plate, it calls for his own individual achievement. It's the individual's time to hit that ball. Baseball is a team sport, yet requires independent action and independent accomplishment by each critical member of the team. If the third baseman doesn't hustle to get that grounder, and doesn't charge that ball and make the throw to first base, then things aren't going to work out.

In a team situation, each individual player needs to perform at the individual level as well as at the team level. Rowans are interested in reaching the goal, getting that man out at first; they know that they need to go the extra step by supporting other members on the team to reach the goal.

Supervision is the task of assigning responsibility. Assigning responsibility involves taking a risk. So let's face it, both the supervisor and the employee are taking risks when a project is assigned.

As a manager, supervisor, or executive, you have to empower your subordinates to be willing to take risks. Let's use that baseball analogy: if a player gets up there, but is not willing to take any risks, he's not going to swing at anything! There's nothing worse than having the official scorekeeper write down a backward "k" in the scorebook. It means you struck out without even swinging. Ouch.

I offer a word of caution here about some people in a supervisory role. There are managers who want to be surrounded by inadequate individuals. The worst ones will even try to chase away competent people because they are trying to protect their own turf. As soon as you see that, you'd better make a change! In fact, you should notice that problem even before it develops because, already, chances are pretty good that they would not have been doing their job to your standards and expectations. They don't have the right character to start with! Rowan-type supervisors are NOT afraid to supervise subordinates who are competent and capable workers.

At the same time, Rowan-type employees want a strong leader as their manager or supervisor. To be sure, that's one of the reasons managers with strong leadership skills are always getting the job done. They attract and keep Rowan-type individuals in their department. Rowans don't like working with people who are not competent. They get aggravated by it! They quit and go someplace else to work! And, quite frankly, who can blame them?

A Different Set of Eyes

Keep this in mind too if you're fortunate enough to have a Rowan working for you: sure, they'll likely get the job done. But another strong advantage to such a person is their ability to provide their own unique, front-line, clear-eyed perspective on a problem. Multiple viewpoints will assist you in obtaining the solutions that will put your business ahead of the others. Sometimes the best answers are so obvious that you can't see them. Sometimes, as we all know, the trees you're studying so closely start to get in the way of the forest. And sometimes you just need someone to point out the obvious.

You can't be afraid to ask for help. If you have never lost anything, then you don't understand this. But if you have lost something, and you have had someone help you find it, then you understand.

It is like when you can't find your glasses. You go into a room and you're looking all over for them, but can't find them anywhere! You call your wife, your son…anybody! And you say, "I need another set of eyes! I can't find my glasses!" Sometimes they're sitting on top of your head, sometimes they're in your hand, sometimes they're right in front of you, and you still can't see them! It's only because sometimes we lose our perspective … on anything.

Mentoring

One of the most important things that should be the responsibility of any manager is to be mentoring someone. One of your main jobs as a manager is to replace yourself so you can move up or expand your department. People who don't understand that, and aren't willing to make that happen, should _not_ be in leadership positions. They have to know that they are accountable for their recommendation. They have to recommend good, competent people, and when they don't, that individual's lack of success reflects on the manager's ability to do his job.

Therefore, if you, as the employer, twist it around a little bit and actually enforce those types of principles and practices, you'll have developed a sound way to encourage and train your own subordinates to seek out and pull other Rowans along.

Personally, I only want people who are smarter than me working for me. Why? Because if they are not smarter than me, then I'm not gaining anything by involving them in my business. A good manager, a good leader, is going to want people who are at the top of their game.

But be careful.

Avoiding Burnout

Rowans, by their very nature, are always willing to take on more and more assignments. As much as that is certainly desirable on the surface, it can also raise a little yellow flag. You have to be cautious of burnout. To put it another way, you as a manager almost have to protect them from themselves.

In business today, with our multiple ways of communicating with one another, our work doesn't always end at the end of the business day. The emails keep going back and forth, just as do the texts—on days off and in the evenings! For that reason, one of the things I always tell the people that are in these key positions is, unless I'm asking them specifically to respond right away, or that it's urgent, I don't expect them to even read any of my emails they receive after business hours. I always tell them that I'm just putting it at the top of your queue for when you get into work next.

I add further that, if it is something that I really need to talk to you about, something that's genuinely urgent, I'll be sure to identify it that way, or perhaps with a phone call instead of a text or an email. At the same time, when Rowan-type people send me emails after hours, I'll either not respond to them, so as not to get it rolling, or I'll respond to them with "Let's go over this in the morning." If I'm the one initiating an email to someone during those times, I generally start it with "In the morning, let's go over this."

You know, it would be nice if you could just leave it alone completely, right? I try to, but often enough, it's really not possible to ignore it completely. Nonetheless, having limits on when you expect them to engage in their off-time is important. If nothing else, it'll temper the fear that you will burn them out, both your fear and theirs.

A Rowan has to be able to balance work hours and non-work hours. It's critical to preventing burnout. It doesn't mean there can't be times when you are working really long days or for very long periods of time. But it does mean that you need to make sure they understand that you see it as important that they take care of themselves, particularly in this regard.

As a manager, especially with a Rowan on your staff, you have to make sure they go home. That is, you have to make sure they don't allow themselves to work seven days a week. You must build into the process, not just opportunity for recognition, but opportunities for recreation as well.

For example, one of the things we always did when we had new hires was to take them out to a local pizza place, with everyone sitting at one table sharing pizza and salad. The managers and supervisors were invited as well, along with key Rowan-like people who were working for us. And we had one big rule at these events: no one is allowed to talk about business. They can talk about work…but not about business! Talk about the funny things that happen at work and stuff like that. And thank God there were plenty of them!

Then we'd tell everyone on those evenings, "If they have any suggestions on how we do something, or how we should do them differently, or how we should do things better, or what we're doing right or wrong, we definitely want to hear them! But, we just *don't* want to hear them tonight." That gives us a little bit of an opportunity to do that, but when it's appropriate, without interfering with the time just to relax and enjoy one another's co-workers. We always encouraged everybody to learn to divide their day into equal parts for rest, for vocation, and also for their family.

A genuine Rowan has to be able to do that. They must be able to leave their troubles at the door when they come into work, and then leave their troubles at work when they go through their door at home. Those who cannot do that will quickly be overwhelmed, and can burn themselves out in a heartbeat.

We've all seen it; we just have to know how to recognize it and prevent it.

Authority

Another aspect of a Rowan's character is that they feel compelled to seize authority. As a manager, you may be anxious to have a project developed, and so decide to place a Rowan in charge of it.

But be careful. That can be very dangerous. You can't put people in charge of supervising others in a project if, in fact, they themselves haven't yet acquired the skills required for the completion of that project. They'll very much want to meet the deadline you have set, but they'll be significantly tethered if you haven't given them the time to get up to speed on the skill requirements of the task. That seemingly minor omission can easily turn against the whole enterprise.

Take the time necessary to bring a potential supervisor, especially a Rowan, up to speed on those skills required for a given task. In that way, they'll more easily begin to comprehend the uniqueness of the situation (timing, dynamics, personalities), and

233

that alone will go a long way toward helping them manage others with those same skill sets. Supervisors need to have a reasonable appreciation of what their subordinates have to go through in order to get their jobs done, so that supervisor and worker are not in conflict with one another.

Let's face it. Learning the skills of a particular project, and being able to lead the organization on that same project, can certainly be confusing at times.

Because Rowans have a take-charge character, they sometimes can exceed their authority, or exceed the mandate of the strategic mission as it's outlined.

When Rowan went to Cuba, his job was to carry a message, and then to carry a message back. His role wasn't to go, and then decide that he should assassinate General Garcia because he wasn't as much of a democratic free-thinker as he thought the U.S. would want him to be.

So what am I saying here? I'm saying that, even a Rowan has to stay within the strategic initiative being put forward. Sometimes, for instance, when there is a shift in strategy, perhaps involving the manner of execution, even a Rowan is sometimes incapable of transcending to the new pattern. That can be a serious problem.

I would classify five-star General Douglas MacArthur (1880-1964) as a quintessential Rowan. His authority level in the Pacific Theater during WWII became completely open-ended, allowing him to make all strategic decisions with regard to Japan after the close of the war. As a seemingly natural consequence, at the beginning of the Korean War in 1950, he was appointed commander of UN military forces in South Korea, while retaining his command of Allied forces in Japan.

But there's the red flag. One of the most difficult things to do to a subordinate is to change his authority level, particularly when that authority is reduced, not increased. Don't ever block their path to ambition, or you may lose your Rowan.

MacArthur pressed for permission to bomb Chinese bases in Manchuria, but President Truman refused such permission. So finally, after MacArthur had made the dispute public, Truman removed MacArthur from command in April of 1951. And therein lies the confusing difficulty. MacArthur was originally put in command of a military exercise, essentially given absolute authority over that theater of operations, and then expected to be limited in that same authority.

More to our business environment: if an employee has been given authority to make expenditure determinations, or hiring

235

or firing determinations, and all of a sudden has her authority restricted, it raises considerable tension and difficulties. It becomes even more difficult when she is no longer doing the tactical work. All of a sudden you are going to restrict their strategic abilities.

I think MacArthur said something like, "I have never known a commander who was given materials or units to use and then told that he cannot use them." I think he also said, "I don't know how I can be ordered to bomb only one end of a bridge!" Who's to say what was the best course of action in that peninsula in those days? What we can say, however, is that there was only one chain of command, and he was not at the top of that chain even though he had been allowed to function as the top of it for many years prior to that.

The lesson here? Rowans always have to be reminded that they may not be at the head of the chain of command. Don't let them think they are, and then pull them back.

First Impressions

The first interaction that a supervisor may have with a Rowan is during the orientation and training of new hires. You never know when you hire a person, or a group of people, if you will find a Rowan. So you should always assume that you may have one in your new hires.

We once hired twenty-five new staffers. Out of that group, there were certainly a lot of them capable of being Rowans. There were quite a few, in fact, who wanted to be Rowans, especially on that first day.

But, they may have gotten their head bitten off by some supervisor one day in the training session. Or they may somehow have interpreted the teaching of something they already knew as being demeaning. Whatever it was, a fair number of them lost that drive, that desire to move forward; or they may have decided this was just not the place for them, and so they never returned the next day.

Rowan is something that's inside a person. You can't get rid of it. Some people will have it no matter what happens to them. They get knocked down, so they get back up and try it again. And they keep trying it again…and again, and again…almost regardless of how many times they get knocked down. It's that willingness to return that is a Rowan character trait. And in business especially, you have the opportunity to have people who have these qualities.

Let's face it, nobody dies in business like they do in battle. So they have the opportunity to return to it. But, to be sure, some of them eventually lose it simply because their actions have been unwelcomed so many times over and over. They finally give up. For my part, I honestly think the potential is out there for a lot more people than you'd think to manifest those rare qualities of a genuine Rowan employee.

I will admit that it is rare to find fully developed Rowans just off the street. But I think it is even rarer to be able to develop it in someone. At some point, though, it is almost basic human nature to have those qualities.

It's like the first day of school. Every student starts with a clean slate, and every student hopes for success. Every student has the drive and the desire. After the first day, though, things seem to change when they realize that they actually have to do the work to get there.

"Oh, I really have to study the stuff?"

"Oh, I have to develop the skills?"

There are all kinds of things. But the desire, the drive to succeed, at least at the start, is there. The key for you as an employer, or as a manager, is to try to find ways to accommodate those individuals in a manner that allows you to extract that Rowan-type character.

That's not always easy. I certainly hate to compare people to pets, but sometimes I think I like my dog more than I like a lot of people. I don't dislike anybody.

There's an expression that goes, "There are no bad dogs, just bad owners." In a legitimate business, there are no bad people. Some just need to be motivated a different way; some are just there for the paycheck, and probably some don't care because they never cared. But…there are no bad dogs.

Chapter 17—How to Keep a "Rowan"

Someone who is truly a Rowan doesn't really give a rat's ass whether he gets rewarded or not. For him, doing a good job is its own reward. In fact, the best reward would be for him to receive an even more challenging assignment, one that would require an even greater degree of creative problem-solving skills.

Do they need to be rewarded differently? No, they themselves don't have that need. But, as their manager, YOU need to reward them differently. And this can become a rather serious issue if you don't recognize their innate need to be challenged.

Issue Challenges

My recommendation in this regard is that you develop some long-range plans, ideas that will carry your business into the future, or maybe ones that are of special personal interest. Then, when you spot a Rowan in your company looking like they are bored, or not performing up to their regular level, give them one of the topics you have developed as a side assignment to work on. Don't make this a high-priority project, but ask them only to look into it when they get their primary assignment finished.

This will do two things. First, it will encourage them to complete the task they are currently involved with. Secondly, it will also get them using their creative skills again, and that is a reward in itself. Boredom for a Rowan doesn't come about because of the labors of the task, but rather because of a lack of opportunity to exercise themselves.

Appreciate Your People

Every successful business knows that it must show its employees that they are appreciated if they are going to keep morale up. Besides giving people a financial reward, there are other ways of doing this.

I know this may sound trite, but we always had a lot of food available. In our break area, there were always boxes of donuts or bagels. During the summer months, we'd barbecue one day a week for everybody, and, at other times, we'd provide pizza when it was too cold to cook outside. We always tried to get those little forced breaks throughout the day where people could have a chance to reset themselves. It's difficult to schedule spontaneity, but it is something that I always tried to infuse into the culture of my business.

One of the best ways we used to do this, at least at our headquarters where we had about 100 employees, was to get a birthday cake for everybody on their birthday. With a hundred people, there was a birthday pretty much every week, and sometimes several during a week. There was always a birthday cake. We didn't stop and sing happy birthday, but people did always stop and comment about whose name was written on the cake.

I know this sounds very trivial, sounds like one of those little things—oh, yeah, so what? But I've learned that many times it's the little things that make the biggest differences. And, ahem, isn't that what this book is all about? We've all heard it: "If you take care of the little things, the big things take care of themselves." To a certain extent I think that the most valuable tool you can use to maintain morale, believe it or not, is food.

Yeah, I know there are always those who feel, "I can get my own lunch; I can get my own food!" But that's not the idea. It's communal food that everybody is sharing in. Besides, this can be extra important to Rowans! They tend to get wrapped up in a project, y'know. Remember, you have to look out for them because they can overdo it.

So we provided donuts or some kind of pastry every

morning, and a lunch every day for all our staff. To be sure, we always supplied plenty of healthy items—fruits and vegetables and such—but made sure to throw in a couple plates of cookies as well. We were always amazed and delighted how many informal meetings genuinely got things done in that lunchroom over a cup of coffee and a cookie or two. People will come together for meetings because it's required. But you really take the edge off of a meeting when everyone knows it's going to be comfortably informal…and include a couple of snacks. In fact, it was often just these types of meetings that ended up being the really productive ones.

As a course of business, we also always do a Christmas party, company picnic, and a circus outing for employees and their families. This is especially important to the family members of those Rowans who work for us, because it lets them know that the company appreciates the time that they miss out on with that person when they are at work. At those events, we take pictures of everybody who's there and put them up on a big bulletin board.

"Morale maintenance" is probably the subject of a whole other book. No one is ever going to get that one exactly right for everyone, because sometimes it seems patronizing, sometimes it seems imposing, and sometimes it is very difficult to put into words.

As an example, we once took all of our managers and above to a party at one of the casinos hosted by *HOUR* magazine, with whom we used to do a lot of advertising. This was a huge event, and we bought tickets for everyone who was on that level of management. We gave them a choice. They could take two tickets, or they could take one ticket and $100, or they could just take the $100 if they didn't want the ticket. Just about everyone involved took the two tickets, and I remember well what a doggone good time we all had! And I'll add that, even the few who didn't take the tickets themselves, did nonetheless take the offer as a form of appreciation that allowed them to take an extra breath that day and feel a little bit better about work.

I won't dwell on these aspects of keeping up a high-spirited, cohesive work force because these are really the fun things to do as a corporate executive or business owner. These are the things that don't really take work. Sure, they take some effort, but stuff that's as enjoyable as these various practices and events are…well, to me they're not really "work."

CONCLUSION

In the introduction to this book, I told you a story about a horseshoe and a nail, and the sudden tumbling down of a once-mighty kingdom. This is the children's rhyme from which I first heard the tale.

For Want of a Nail

For want of a nail the shoe was lost.
For want of a shoe the horse was lost.
For want of a horse the rider was lost.
For want of a rider the message was lost.
For want of a message the battle was lost.
For want of a battle the kingdom was lost.
And all for the want of a horseshoe nail.

Although its original author is unknown, there have been variations of this insightful little story attributed to many great men.

One story dates it to August 22, 1485 during the decisive Battle of Bosworth Field. It was the battle wherein King Richard III himself was struck, and fell from his horse. And, as recounted by William Shakespeare, the fallen king then famously cried out, *A horse, a horse! My kingdom for a horse*!

As it turned out, unfortunately, there was no horse for the poor king, and moments latter he lay dead in the field.

The story is short and simple, isn't it? It's certainly a very small thing to dwell on, wouldn't you say?

But isn't that just the point of this entire book? My hope in bringing it to your attention once again, and especially here at the close of our journey together, is simply to emphasize that you constantly keep at the front of your mind how true it is that BIG THINGS HAVE SMALL BEGINNINGS…for better or worse, … and even for kings.

Now, let's face it, if you have been in business—even for only a few days—you already know well that there is also always the unexpected, some giant oak tree that will fall across your path just so it can keep you up at night. Sometimes it'll be a pesky government regulation. It could also be the current economic conditions. Maybe you're having to grapple with health and family issues while you scramble about juggling the challenges of your business. We have all been there, haven't we? And, if you haven't…well, you will be.

But please take courage and understand a very important principle. The great game is not just a single roll of the dice. Never!

In this amazing country of ours, there is always a seat waiting for you at the next table. The trick is not to mind that it hurts when you get knocked down. Just pick yourself up, dust yourself off, and start all over again.

The strength, the courage, the perseverance it takes to pick yourself up time and time again, to my mind at least, comes from having a good family and a good support group. That's the absolute key. Turn the page for my own quick example...

Members of my Masonic Lodge (above) are almost like my extended family and are certainly part of my support group

I know. I've been knocked down more than a couple of times, and not just to my knees. I've been knocked flat on my face too many times to count.

BUT…that's not what this book is about!

This book is NOT about failing. This book is about preventing, limiting, and continually overcoming the small "failures"—obstacles, if you will—that pop up whenever we set out to accomplish something big. We're not dwelling on a failure here and there in these chapters. We're talking about achieving success, and success in no small measure.

As you embark on this journey, always remember that every event in life is a lot like a coin with two sides. One side is good, and the other side is bad. It's up to us to find the good side. It's always there, but you gotta look for it. The good news? The BIG news? You can keep flipping that coin until you get what you want.

We have all experienced some adversities in our lives. We can choose to handle them in one of two ways. The first way is that we can learn from them. That is, we can grow in our understanding of things, and thereby advance our body of knowledge. This path will most assuredly lead to the continual growth and improvement of our character.

Or, we can slide into self-pity. That's the second way to handle adversity, and one that I strongly urge you to reject out of hand.

The lesson of the black and white mosaic pavement, checkered, as it might be seen, with both good and bad, is truly a life lesson. It is up to us—to you and to me—to decide our own destiny.

My life has been blessed with both good and bad, and yet, from every setback, I have enjoyed some of the most wonderful things that this life can offer.

When I was 17 years old, I was shot during a robbery. A quarter-inch difference in the bullet's path, and my life would have ended. I can tell you today that that was bad. So you might ask, sooo, what's the good side of that coin, right?

Well, here it is.

From that one near-tragic incident, I very quickly became alive and alert to the incredibly fragile nature of life, and also developed a much greater awareness of my surroundings… everywhere and anywhere. I have become very situationally aware and observant. I know too that this experience also shaped many of the political views that I hold to this day.

And you know what? I can still feel the bullet lodged in the back of my skull. Yeah, it was too dangerously close to some critical nerve and brain matter for them to attempt its removal. So I suppose I always had that option to bellyache about it, maybe to get all fired-up angry about it, or maybe to go into a little scared depression. But I'm glad to say that I never did. Instead, in fact, even today, I choose to think of it as a lucky charm.

Allow me to offer just one more example.

When my first marriage ended in divorce, I thought it was the worst thing that could have happened to me. But it wasn't! Not by a long shot.

In time, I eventually came to know and marry the love of my life, my wife Mi, as a result of that divorce.

During the first years of our marriage, we struggled to have children. Normally a bad side of the coin, right? But, no, it wasn't, as it turned out. In fact, it resulted in us adopting our Aaron, a son who has brought such joy to my life that, as I write this now, I find it impossible to find words adequate to express it.

We went on to have three more sons: Brandon, Bradley, and Wesley III. And I can only tell you that, together with my wife, those four wonderful boys are…well…my whole reason for being. And yet none of my sons would be in my life at all if not for the "blessing," as it turned out, of that early divorce.

I have honestly come to believe that true wealth is measured in your children.

As I look back at it all now, I can honestly tell you that, in business, every success I enjoyed was the result of a previous setback. And it's precisely because of that that I tell you, there is good in every experience that life has to offer, and it is our responsibility to seek out that good and advance to the next square on that checkerboard of life. At times it may be difficult to see our next step. And surely, sometimes things may seem to go from bad to worse. But I urge you to keep moving forward, particularly in the ugly face of adversity. The path to happiness is well-marked; we just have to be willing to keep looking for it.

Kipling in London in 1895

We've come now to the end of our journey. Allow me, therefore, to close our discussion by leaving you with my all-time favorite poem, one by the great Rudyard Kipling. He put into words so much more eloquently than I ever could, many of the same principles that I have been talking with you about in this book.

Kipling called it simply *If*. And yet he offers the most brilliant and illustrative treatise on embracing both success and failure as one. These are words that I have tried my very best to live by. I've shared his words many times with my sons, as these words have become very dear to me. It is my sincere hope, therefore, dear reader, that you too might find them as powerful and inspirational as I have.

If—

BY RUDYARD KIPLING

If you can keep your head when all about you
    Are losing theirs and blaming it on you,
If you can trust yourself when all men doubt you,
    But make allowance for their doubting too;
If you can wait and not be tired by waiting,
    Or being lied about, don't deal in lies,
Or being hated, don't give way to hating,
    And yet don't look too good, nor talk too wise:

If you can dream—and not make dreams your master;
If you can think—and not make thoughts your aim;
If you can meet with Triumph and Disaster
    And treat those two impostors just the same;
If you can bear to hear the truth you've spoken
    Twisted by knaves to make a trap for fools,
Or watch the things you gave your life to, broken,
    And stoop and build 'em up with worn-out tools:

If you can make one heap of all your winnings
    And risk it on one turn of pitch-and-toss,
And lose, and start again at your beginnings
    And never breathe a word about your loss;
If you can force your heart and nerve and sinew
    To serve your turn long after they are gone,
And so hold on when there is nothing in you
    Except the Will which says to them: 'Hold on!'

If you can talk with crowds and keep your virtue,
    Or walk with Kings—nor lose the common touch,
If neither foes nor loving friends can hurt you,
    If all men count with you, but none too much;
If you can fill the unforgiving minute
    With sixty seconds' worth of distance run,
Yours is the Earth and everything that's in it,
    And—which is more—you'll be a Man, my son

If there is a take-away from all of this, reader, it is this: whatever you want to accomplish, it is up to YOU. It is up to you alone to become the person who has the willingness to do what it takes to achieve the success you desire. It is up to YOU to build within yourself the determination and the positive attitude that will guide you safely on the journey that you choose. It is up to you. Always remember that there is no such thing as failure. All setbacks are temporary. The Great Game never ends...unless you decide to quit.

So I urge you, get yourself into the Game, and have the time of your life!

THERE IS NO SUCH THING AS

THE END

By the way, before you put this book down, if you're still struggling to find that "demon" in the painting of "The Prisoner" back on page 141, it's another one of those things that remind us to look closely in order to see all that is really there. It's actually the little demon clutching the prisoner's left leg, indicated in the drawing below.

But don't feel bad. It took me about six months of staring at the intriguing little painting until I finally found it myself.

But, hey…thanks for playing.

Wes

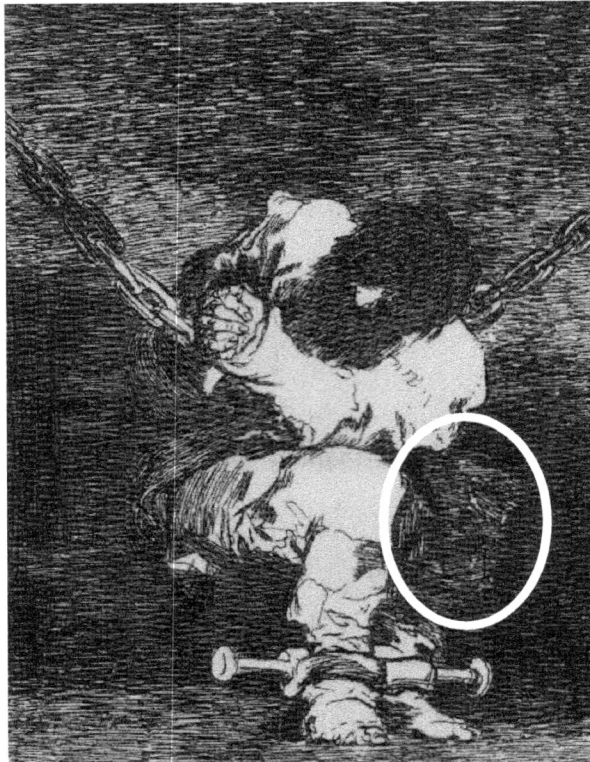

About The Author

Wes Berry is a Keynote Speaker and Workshop Facilitator with the professional skills and real-life experience to deliver on any stage. He works with Fortune 500 companies like Johnson & Johnson to smaller businesses and associations of all sizes that are seeking a breakthrough experience. Wes changes lives and transforms organizations by delivering a Paradigm Shift. He has written sixteen business and success books and is a *Wall Street Journal* best-selling author and TEDx speaker. As an entrepreneur, he built a $750 million international company that operated in 130 countries.

His business knowledge and communications skills have made him an expert media contributor on many topics, from commercial drone applications to the downsizing of Sears, resulting in appearances with various media outlets. His many media appearances include NPR, *The Wall Street Journal*, *The London Times*, *Entrepreneur* and *Time* magazines, Fox News, Neil Cavuto, Geraldo Rivera, and John Stossel, to name just a few.

Visit his website at WesBerryGroup.com to learn more.